HEINEMANN HIS

STUDY UNITS

THE RISE OF ISLAM

Heinemann

John Child

Heinemann Library,
an imprint of Heinemann Publishers (Oxford) Ltd,
Halley Court, Jordan Hill, Oxford OX2 8EJ

OXFORD LONDON EDINBURGH MADRID
ATHENS BOLOGNA PARIS MELBOURNE
SYDNEY AUCKLAND SINGAPORE TOKYO
IBADAN NAIROBI HARARE GABORONE
PORTSMOUTH NH (USA)

First published 1993

95 96 97 98 99 00 10 9 8 7 6 5 4 3 2 1

**British Library Cataloguing in Publication Data is available
from the British Library on request.**

ISBN 0–431–07365–1 (Paperback)

Designed by Ron Kamen, Green Door Design Ltd, Basingstoke

Illustrated by Jeff Edwards

Printed in China

The front cover shows a tile mosaic at the Mosque of Sidi
Sahab, Kairouan.

Acknowledgements

The author and publisher would like to thank the following for
permission to reproduce photographs:

J. Allan Cash Ltd: 5.1E
Ancient Art & Architecture Collection: 1.2B, 2.1A,
3.1D, 3.2D
Bibliothèque Nationale: 3.5F
Bibliothèque Nationale/Islamic Foundation: 3.6B
Bollinger/Stern: 5.3D
C. M. Dixon: cover, 3.1B, 3.10B, 3.11A, 3.11C, 4.1A,
5.1A, 5.1B
Werner Forman Archive/National Museum of Anthropology,
Madrid: 3.2B
Girandon: 1.2A, 3.7D, 4.3A, 4.4B, 5.2A
Girandon/Bibliothèque National: 3.8C
Girandon/Bridgeman: 4.2B
Sonia Halliday Photographs: 1.2D, 3.3E, 3.8B, 3.9B, 3.9C,
3.10A, 3.11D, 3.12A, 4.1B, 4.2A, 4.6D, 5.1D

Robert Harding Picture Library: 1.2C, 2.5A, 3.2C,
3.7B, 3.10C, 3.12G, 4.5B
Michael Holford: 2.4A
Hutchinson Library: 3.4D, 5.1F
Islamic Foundation: 5.3C
Kobal Collection: 3.4C
The Metropolitan Museum: 3.8A
Christine Osborne: 2.5C
Picturepoint Ltd: 5.2C
Private Collection: 4.6A
Peter Sanders: 5.2B
Syndication International: 3.12F
Wayland Publishers Ltd: 3.8D
Jeremy Whitaker: 3.12H

We are also grateful to the following for permission to
reproduce copyright material:

The Muslim Educational Trust for Source 5.3B, taken from
Islam, Beliefs and Teachings by the Muslim Educational Trust,
1984.

Every effort has been made to contact copyright holders of
material reproduced in this book. Any omissions will be
rectified in subsequent printings if notice is given to the
publisher.

Thanks also to Dr Ahsan of the Islamic Foundation.

Details of written sources

In some sources the wording or sentence structure has been
simplified to ensure that the source is accessible.

M. Bianco, *Gadafi, Voice of the Desert*, Longman, 1975: 5.3A
Wilfrid Blunt, *The Splendours of Islam*, Viking Press, 1976:
3.1C, 3.11E
Hermann Bondi (Ed.), *The Rise of Islam*, Marshall Cavendish,
1969: 2.1B, 4.2C, 4.6B
R. Bruce, *Muhammad*, Holt, Rinehart and Winston, 1984:
2.2B
R. Bruce, *Islamic Worship*, Cassell, 1985: 5.1C
Trevor Cairns, *Barbarians, Christians and Muslims*, Cambridge
University Press, 1971: 2.3D
Brian Catchpole, *The Clash of Cultures*, Heinemann
Educational, 1981: 3.5E
P. W. Gardner, R. Bateman, *Core Skills in History Two*, Holmes
McDougall, 1989: 3.12B
Rosalyn Kendrick, *Islam*, Heinemann Educational, 1989: 2.2C,
2.3C, 2.4A, 2.5B, 3.5B, 3.9D
Peter Mansfield, *The Arabs*, Penguin, 1976: 2.3A
Joyce Milton, Raphael Steinberg, Sarah Lewis, *Religion at the
Crossroads*, Cassell, 1980: 4.2D, 4.3A, 4.4A, 4.6C
Malise Ruthven, *Islam in the World*, Penguin, 1984: 2.2D
Paul Shuter, John Child, David Taylor, *Skills in History*, Book
2, Heinemann Educational, 1989: 3.5D
Desmond Stewart, *Early Islam*, Time-Life Books, 1967: 3.3A,
3.3B, 3.4A, 3.5C, 3.6A
Richard Tames, *The Muslim World*, MacDonald, 1982: 3.5A
Hugh Thomas, *Spain*, Time-Life Books, 1964: 3.11B
W. Montgomery Watt, *The Majesty that was Islam*, Sidgwick
and Jackson, 1974: 2.4C, 2.5E, 3.3E
Gavin Young, *Iraq, Land of Two Rivers*, Collins, 1980: 3.3D,
3.4B

CONTENTS

1.1 The Impact of Islam (1)

Islam is one of the world's most important religions. Followers of Islam are called **Muslims.**

Islam was started in Arabia by the **Prophet Muhammad.** He was a man who lived from 570 to 632. The first Muslims were **Arabs** and they conquered nearby countries, spreading Islam amongst other people. Large parts of the world came under Arab and Muslim control.

The map below shows Muslim rule at its greatest. As the Arabs spread, taking their religion with them, they learned from the people they conquered. They wrote down what they learned in books, which were read all over the Muslim world. Then they worked to improve that knowledge. They became very advanced in art, architecture, science and mathematics. They built splendid towns like Baghdad, Damascus, Cairo and Cordoba. Many features of modern Muslim countries began then. Even countries further away, like Britain, learned a lot from the Muslims. The numbering system which we all use today came to western Europe from the Muslim world.

Islam in AD 750

BRITAIN

EUROPE

SPAIN
Cordoba

TURKEY

SYRIA
Damascus · Baghdad   PERSIA

MOROCCO   MEDITERRANEAN SEA

Cairo

EGYPT

ARABIA
The birthplace of Muhammad

AFRICA

☐ Muslim lands
☐ Byzantine Empire

0   500   1000 miles
0   800   1600 km

Islam in the world today

The worldwide distribution of Muslims today

- over 85%
- over 50%
- over 20%
- over 5%
- over 1%
- less than 1%

ATLANTIC OCEAN
USSR
EUROPE
YUGOSLAVIA
BULGARIA
TURKEY
ASIA
MOROCCO
TUNISIA
ALBANIA
LEBANON
SYRIA
ISRAEL
IRAQ
IRAN
AFGHANISTAN
JORDAN
ALGERIA
LIBYA
EGYPT
KUWAIT
PAKISTAN
WESTERN SAHARA
QATAR
UAE
SAUDI ARABIA
MAURITANIA
OMAN
INDIA
MALI
NIGER
CHAD
SUDAN
SOUTH YEMEN
NORTH YEMEN
DJIBOUTI
UPPER VOLTA
GUINEA
NIGERIA
ETHIOPIA
SOMALIA
IVORY COAST
CAMEROON
UGANDA
BENIN
GHANA

MALAYSIA
BORNEO
NEW GUINEA
SUMATRA
INDONESIA
CELEBES
JAVA

| 0 | 500 | 1000 miles |
| 0 | 800 | 1600 km |

Later, Arab control weakened. From about 1050 the Muslims around the Mediterranean fell under the control of new rulers, the **Turks.** They were also Muslims and spread Islam even further. At first, this was also a splendid empire, but from about 1700 the Turkish Empire became weak and started to break up. For all of this time Islam was the main religion in the area.

Eventually, in 1918, the Turkish Empire was split up into smaller countries. Saudi Arabia, Iran, Iraq and Egypt are just some of the modern Muslim countries which used to be in the Arab and Turkish Empires. They are very important countries in the modern world.

Today there are over 1,100 million Muslims. The teachings and history of Islam affect the way they think and act. Muslims are scattered throughout the world: only one sixth are Arabs and over two million Muslims live in Britain. The expansion of Islam had a huge impact on the world in the past; Islam has a vital part to play in the world today.

Muhammad

Muhammad (570–632) was born into a humble family. His father, Abdullah, had died suddenly, leaving his new bride, Amina, pregnant. Muhammad was raised by his uncle, Abu Talib, a merchant. He first worked as a shepherd, then as a merchant on his uncle's trade caravans.

Muhammad was 40 years old before he received a revelation from the Angel Gabriel. During the rest of his life, he continued to receive messages from God. These messages formed the beliefs of Islam. First his friends and then the tribes of Arabia were converted to Islam. Later it spread across huge areas.

Muhammad fell ill in Medina in 632. He had a fever and violent headaches. For several days he was nursed by his wife, Ayesha. Finally, his head cradled in Ayesha's arms, the Prophet Muhammad died.

1.2 Sources

This book is about the way Islam grew and about the countries where the Muslims lived. It is about Muhammad, who started Islam, and his life and teaching. It is about the way the followers of Muhammad, first Arabs and then Turks, conquered huge areas of land, thus spreading the religion of Islam. It is about the towns they built over a thousand years ago, their buildings, laws, clothes, crafts, art, trade, ships, schools and medicine. It is about the battles they fought to gain and keep control of their land.

But how do we know about all of this? What is the evidence for what is written in this book?

Historians use two types of evidence: primary sources and secondary sources.

A **primary source** is evidence which comes from the time of the events being studied. We have many types of primary sources of evidence about the Islamic world. Some are **written** in Arabic, like the medical books of Arab doctors. Sometimes, travellers who went to Muslim lands would write about what they saw. Other primary sources are not written. They are called **artefacts**, things people have made. For example, some buildings survive from the time of early Muslim rule. So does some pottery, tile decorations, paintings, coins and jewellery. Weapons, clothes and carpets from one thousand years ago are very rare however.

Secondary sources are produced later by people who have studied the primary evidence and other secondary sources and come up with their own interpretations of the past. This textbook is a secondary source of evidence about the Islamic world.

A

SOURCE

A medical book by a Muslim doctor showing the workings of the eye, probably 10th century.

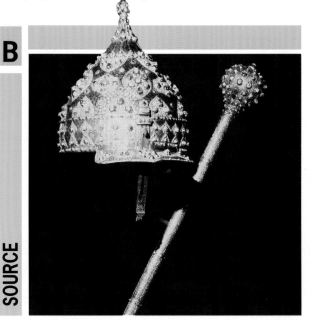

B

SOURCE

Jewelled golden helmet and mace, used by a Turkish sultan in the 16th century.

The Dome of the Rock. A 7th century mosque (place of worship) built by Muslims in Jerusalem.

SOURCE

D

SOURCE

Ibn Khaldun

Ibn Khaldun (1332–1406) was an Arab Muslim historian. He lived in the 14th century and researched the rise of Islam. His books show that he realized historians cannot always take their sources at face value. In 1380 he wrote in his book *Al-Muqaddima*, 'The history writer needs many sources and varied knowledge; he also needs keen judgement and careful scrutiny to lead him to the truth and away from errors. If reliance is placed on simple information without studying its circumstances there will be a danger of straying from the right path.'

A 16th century miniature painting showing Turkish Muslims building a castle during the time of Sultan Murad III (ruled 1574–95).

2.1 Muhammad – his Early Life

Arabia was a very poor area, mostly desert or scrub. Many Arabs made a living from tending sheep. Some of these were **bedouins** who were nomads, constantly moving their sheep, camels and tents from place to place. Others used camels in groups, called **caravans**, to carry goods from town to town to sell. The Arabs were split into many tribes. There was no single king who ruled them. They had no single religion either. Most Arabs worshipped several gods and spirits that they believed lived in rocks and trees.

Muhammad was born in 570 in **Mecca*** (Makkah), a trading town on the caravan routes. It had the country's most sacred temple, a cube shaped building called the **Ka'ba**. The Ka'ba had over 360 altars, statues and other religious objects or idols which the Arabs worshipped. People travelled many miles to worship there.

Muhammad belonged to an important tribe, the **Koraish**, (Quraysh). They charged fees to all the traders and worshippers who came to Mecca. But Muhammad was an orphan by the age of six and quite poor. He worked on the caravans. He disliked life in Mecca. There was too much fighting and greed among the tribes; women, children and the poor were badly treated; there was too much drunkenness and gambling; people worshipped all kinds of idols. From about 610 Muhammad spent more time alone, thinking and praying on nearby Mount Hira. Then he started to get messages from God. Muhammad told his friends about the messages. He called them **revelations**; truths revealed to him by God. Straight away some people wrote them down. Eventually they were collected together in a book called the **Koran** (Qur'an).

In the revelations, an angel said that Muhammad was the last of God's prophets (messengers) and more important than those before, like Jesus. Muhammad began to preach these messages to the people. He said there was only one God (the Arabic for God is **Allah**); that it was evil to worship idols; that greed was wrong; that Allah would judge everyone when they died and send them to Heaven or Hell; that God's followers should obey Him before all others. Islam means submission (to God's will).

Arabia at the time of the birth of Muhammad

BYZANTINE EMPIRE
PERSIA
MEDITERRANEAN SEA
Damascus
Baghdad
Cairo
Medina
Mecca
RED SEA
ARABIA
PERSIAN GULF
INDIAN OCEAN

miles
0   250   500
0   400   800
km

— Major trade route

Muhammad gained many followers, especially among the poor. But Islam was not popular with the rich in Mecca. They feared losing their money, their religions and their power. In 622 many Muslims began to move away from Mecca to settle in **Medina** (Madinah), a nearby town. In Medina, the Muslims were welcomed. Eventually, Muhammad also left for Medina, chased by the Koraish. They offered a prize of 100 camels for his capture. This move to Medina is called the **hijrah**.

The birth of Christ is so important to Christians that they count their dates from then. The hijrah is so important to Muslims that they start counting their history from then. So the year AD 622 is the year 1 AH (After Hijrah) for Muslims.

B

SOURCE

At the dead of night, soldiers burst into the house. They were sent to arrest him as an enemy of the people and a danger to the city. But Muhammad and his friend Abu Bakr slipped away into the desert hills where they hid in a cave.

A modern historian writing in 'The Rise of Islam', 1969.

Khadijah

Khadijah (555–620), first wife of Muhammad, was a wealthy widow and trader who employed him to work as a business agent for her caravans. They married when he was 25 and she was 40. They were married for 25 years. They had six children, though only four survived. Fatima is the most famous of their children. She supported Muhammad through the difficult years of his revelations and was the first convert to Islam.

A

SOURCE

The Koran is the Muslim book of God's revelations to Muhammad. It is always read aloud in Arabic.

2.2 Muhammad – his Later Life

Muhammad arrived in Medina with several of his followers. The people there welcomed him as the prophet of God and found places in their homes for the Muslims. Muhammad continued to preach and got more followers. He soon became the leader of Medina. People looked to him to solve disputes in the town and with other tribes. He started to arrange collections for the needy. Gradually, he began to make laws for people to follow, including rules about marriage, divorce and food. He was still getting messages from God and these were more and more about how people should lead their lives. For example, Chapter 17 of the Koran includes commands for Muslims to be kind to their parents and the old and to be generous. Islam gave status and the hope of Heaven to the poor; Muhammad's laws brought justice and order. Medina had become a small Islamic state with Muhammad as its leader.

B SOURCE

Permission is given by God to those who are fighting because they have been wronged, they have been driven from their homes for no reason.

The Koran, Chapter 22 (verse 40).

C SOURCE

The Meccans were still determined to harm Muhammad. They tried to bribe the Medinans to hand him over. They persecuted the relatives of the Muslims in Mecca. In 623 a small group of Muslims raided a camel train. Although Muhammad had not planned this attack, he understood their reasons. Sadly it provided the Meccans with an excuse to attack Medina with a full army. Muhammad only had 313 warriors, including young boys. They marched out of the city, determined to die for God if they must. To everyone's amazement, their faith and courage won the day.

From 'Islam' by Rosalyn Kendrick, 1989.

A SOURCE

A painting of the Battle of Badr, painted many years after the event.

A huge force of nearly 1,000 men was sent by the Koraish to escort the next caravan. They then advanced upon Medina. Muhammad chose to make his stand at the water wells of Badr. He had three of the four wells filled in. The tired and thirsty Meccans had to fight for water on ground chosen by their enemies.

From 'Islam in the World', by Malise Ruthven, 1984.

But tension between the Muslims and the Koraish in Mecca continued. The Meccans accused the Muslims of raiding their trade caravans. In 624, the Meccans sent an army of about 1,000 men to punish the Muslims. The Muslims only had a force of 300 but they were very loyal and brave. They won the fight, called the **Battle of Badr**. The Muslims were now a fighting force as well as a religious group. Muhammad made treaties with other Arab tribes to make sure that they didn't join the Meccans. Some of these tribes became Muslims.

Fighting continued for the next few years. Muhammad sometimes led the Muslims in battle; once he was wounded in the face and leg. He was a successful general. Eventually, the Muslims wore down the Meccans and in 630 Muhammad took his followers back to Mecca in triumph. He went directly to the Ka'ba, took out all of the altars and idols and declared it a temple to Allah alone. This was a wise decision since the Ka'ba was known all over Arabia and it became a place of worship for all Muslims. By a mixture of preaching, persuasion and force, the Muslims soon controlled all of the main tribes and towns of Arabia.

Muhammad became ill in 632 and died. In about 23 years he had started a religion which had come to dominate the lives of thousands of followers and was still expanding.

Fatima

Fatima (about 606–32) was the daughter of Muhammad and his first wife, Khadijah. Fatima married Ali, her father's cousin, who was later to become the fourth **caliph** (successor of Muhammad as the leader of Islam). Ali founded the section of Islam called the Shi'ites.

Fatima had two daughters and two sons. The sons, Hasan and Husain, were later involved in wars fought to decide the leadership of Islam.

Fatima is regarded by many Muslims as the ideal woman. Some Muslims believe that Fatima was the product of a virgin birth. Fatima helped to nurse Muhammad through his final illness and died herself only a few months after him.

Muhammad had no sons. From 909, a group called the Fatimids gained control of North Africa. They ruled Egypt for almost 300 years and founded the city of Cairo. They claimed to be descended from the Prophet Muhammad through Fatima.

2.3 Arab Expansion

When Muhammad died, Muslims controlled most of Arabia. Soon they started expanding much further. Why did they do this?

Some Arabs were eager to spread Islam. The Koran promised that any Muslim who died in battle for his religion would go to Heaven. It also said that Allah supported the use of war to defend Muslims against enemies of Islam. Others joined the attacks for the riches they brought. They wanted to expand into the fertile land of the Persian Empire and the Byzantine Empire (the remains of the Roman Empire).

The success of the Arabs was amazing. By 640, moving north, they had captured Jerusalem and Damascus and controlled Syria. Soon after, they conquered Persia. Arab armies also headed west. By 642 these armies captured Cairo and took control of Egypt. A navy was created and Cyprus was captured in 649. By 670 the Arabs had occupied Tunisia and in 708 they reached the Atlantic Ocean. Striking east, they had reached Samarkand by 676 and the borders of India by 707. Victory at the **Battle of Talas** in 751 against the Chinese secured central Asia. From such a humble start, how had they done it? The sources in this unit give some clues.

A SOURCE

The Arab tactics were simple. They would charge the enemy and cast a shower of javelins. They would repeat this until the enemy showed signs of breaking and then start hand to hand combat. They were usually outnumbered and the superiority of their enemies should have been overwhelming. The Arabs had no siege equipment (to help them break down the defences of a city or fortress).

From 'The Arabs' by Peter Mansfield, 1976.

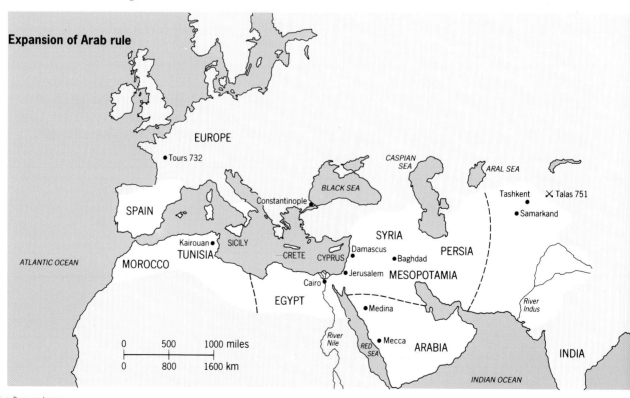

Expansion of Arab rule

EUROPE
• Tours 732
CASPIAN SEA
ARAL SEA
BLACK SEA
Tashkent • ✕ Talas 751
Constantinople • Samarkand
SPAIN
SYRIA
Kairouan • SICILY
TUNISIA
CRETE CYPRUS • Damascus PERSIA
ATLANTIC OCEAN MOROCCO • Baghdad
• Jerusalem MESOPOTAMIA
Cairo •
EGYPT River Indus
• Medina
River Nile
0 500 1000 miles
0 800 1600 km
RED SEA • Mecca ARABIA
INDIA
INDIAN OCEAN

A 10th century bowl from Mesopotamia. It may give us some clues about the weapons of the Muslim soldiers.

C

SOURCE

There were many reasons for this rapid expansion:

- there was white-hot enthusiasm amongst the Muslims. Muhammad inspired great devotion in his people.
- the new faith was vastly superior to the old idol worship of Arabia; this was obvious to any thinking person.
- many Jews and Christians found Islam a more logical and reasonable belief.
- Persia and Byzantium were both weak during this period, having fought each other for some 200 years.
- the ideal Muslim fought with courage and compassion.

From 'Islam' by Rosalyn Kendrick, 1989.

D

SOURCE

Within a few years, they had destroyed the Persian Empire, which had already been weakened by the Byzantines. Against the Byzantines, their task was easier because the people were tired of heavy taxes. They had been persecuted because of differences of opinion about some points of the Christian religion. They expected better treatment from the Muslims. In North Africa the fierce Berbers became Muslims and added new strength to the Arab armies.

The Arabs were tough men. They knew that if they were killed in this holy war, Allah would reward them in paradise. They believed that Allah had decided that Islam would triumph.

From 'Barbarians, Christians and Muslims' by Trevor Cairns, 1971.

Umar

Umar (about 591–644) was the second caliph. When Muhammad died, his closest friend Abu Bakr became the caliph. In 634, Abu Bakr died and Umar became the second caliph.

Umar had been a close adviser to Muhammad. He was a giant of a man, very gentle and religious. Like Muhammad, he lived a very simple life. While he led them, Arab armies conquered huge areas of the Middle East.

When his armies had surrounded Jerusalem, Umar travelled there with one servant and a camel. He entered Jerusalem at the head of a huge army, but he ordered that there should be no killing or stealing. He made sure that Jews and Christians in conquered lands could worship in their own way.

Umar was stabbed to death by a Persian who had a private grudge against him.

2.4 The Rightly-Guided Caliphs

After Muhammad died, in 632, the Muslims needed a new leader – for their country and for Islam, their religion. It was not clear who should take over from Muhammed as leader of the Muslims. A group of Muhammad's closest friends chose Abu Bakr to be their new leader. The Muslims gave him the title of **caliph**, which means successor or deputy. As caliph, Abu Bakr was ruler of the new Muslim territories and defender of the Islamic religion. Abu Bakr was succeeded by three other caliphs – Umar, Uthman and Ali. The first four leaders followed Muhammad's example closely. Like him, they used the rules of Islam to govern the Muslims. They lived simple lives and tried to rule fairly. But their rule was also a time when the Muslims were constantly fighting to make Islam stronger. They encouraged wars and battles against other Arabs and against outsiders, saying they were necessary to remove injustice and the enemies of Islam.

Arabs swearing allegiance to Caliph Ali after the murder of Caliph Uthman. (A painting produced many years after the event.)

B

During the 30 years after 632, the Muslims were governed by four **caliphs**, who were outstanding men chosen for their good character. They were unselfish and tolerant, knew the Koran, and had been Muhammad's dearest friends. The word caliph means successor. These first four caliphs were known as the 'rightly-guided' caliphs because they followed Muhammad's example closely.

Abu Bakr ruled for only two years. He was followed by **Umar**, a giant of a man, from 634–44. When he went to Jerusalem, he set out with only one servant and a camel, which he and the servant took turns to ride. Umar lived all his life without luxuries.

Uthman then became the leader. He was a simple and kind-hearted man. But he angered the people of Egypt by replacing the governor with his own cousin, who set higher taxes. A group of Egyptians killed Uthman in 656.

Ali, the next caliph, was opposed by many Muslims including Uthman's cousin Muawiya. There was constant argument. In 661 Ali was also struck down while at prayer in the mosque. He did not die for three days, during which time he protected and fed his assassin.

SOURCE

From 'Islam' by Rosalyn Kendrick, 1989.

C

At Muhammad's death the gentle, faithful but aged Abu Bakr was appointed caliph. His commanders, with his blessing, set out on a jihad (holy war) against Syria.

Abu Bakr died after reigning only two years. He was followed by the bad-tempered Umar (634–644) then the aged and incompetent Uthman (644–656). Both of these men were killed by angry subjects.

Ali, son-in-law of Muhammad, became the fourth caliph (656–661). But some Muslims wouldn't accept him. Ali spent his entire five-year reign in internal warfare. One of his enemies was Ayesha, Muhammad's widow. In 656, at the Battle of Basra, she was taken prisoner on a battlefield strewn with 13,000 corpses. Ali, always merciful, kept her safe but under guard where she could do him no harm. In 661 he too was killed by an assassin.

SOURCE

Adapted from the work of a modern historian writing in 'The Rise of Islam', 1969.
It is interesting that Muslim accounts of the battle at Basra put the number of deaths at about 6,000.

Abu Bakr

Abu Bakr (about 572–634) was Muhammad's closest friend. He was the second person Muhammad converted to Islam. His wife, Khadijah, was the first. After she died, Muhammad had several wives. One of these was Abu Bakr's daughter, Ayesha.

Abu Bakr travelled with Muhammad when he left Mecca (the hijrah). There is a story that they had to hide in a cave. They were saved when one of the people searching for them turned away from the entrance when he saw that a spider had woven a web across it, and a pigeon had nested in the web.

When Muhammad died Abu Bakr became the first caliph. He was a humble man who hardly looked like a leader. He was portly, with a red beard, and dressed in ragged, patched clothes. When he became the caliph, he told the Muslims, 'People, I have been chosen by you as your leader, though I am no better than you. If I do well, give me support. If I do wrong, set me right!' Under his control, Muslim armies conquered all of Arabia.

He was already 60 years old when he became caliph. He died two years later from a fever.

2.5 Sunni and Shi'ites

The last unit told how the Muslims argued about who should be the caliph. Some supported **Ali.** Ali was Muhammad's closest living relative. He was his cousin and married to his youngest daughter, Fatima. Other Muslims supported **Muawiya,** Uthman's cousin. Muawiya was one of the powerful **Umayyad** family. They were part of the Koraish tribe who first opposed Muhammad. Many of them had only become Muslims just before Muhammad died. Muawiya's supporters said that it was wrong for the leadership of Islam to stay in Muhammad's family. They said that the most able Muslim should be the leader. He should rule by using the Koran and Muhammad's ways (Sunnah). These Muslims were called the **Sunni.**

Ali's supporters said that Muhammad's family should succeed him and that he had trained Ali as his successor. They didn't accept that Abu Bakr, Umar and Uthman had been real caliphs. Some of them cursed them in their chants. They thought that Muawiya and his followers were half-hearted Muslims, more interested in power than Islam. Ali's supporters were called the **Shia Ali** (party of Ali), or **Shi'ites** for short.

When Ali died, his son Husain tried to get the caliphate back for his family. But he was killed in battle and became a Shi'ite **martyr.** (See Source B.)

Shi'ite Muslims at prayer in present-day Iran.

SOURCE A

SOURCE B

In 681, Husain and about 70 men were surrounded at Karbala by an army of 4,000 supporters of Yazid, Muawiya's son. They were close to water but Yazid's army denied them drink. For eight days, they tried to get Husain to give up his claim to be the next caliph, but he refused.

Outnumbered, his followers were killed. When Husain held out his baby son for mercy, an arrow, fired through the baby's neck, pinned him to Husain's arm. At the end, the body of Husain, riddled with arrows, was trampled in the mud. His head was hacked off and taken back to Yazid.

The shrine where Husain was buried at Karbala became a holy place for Shi'ites. They worship there every year and weep for the victory of evil over good. They promise to defend their beliefs as Husain did.

From 'Islam' by Rosalyn Kendrick, 1989.

The Shi'ites never regained control of Islam. There were always many more Sunni. Today, about ten per cent of Muslims are Shi'ites. But they are a powerful minority. Iran is ruled by Shi'ites. Many more Shi'ites live in Pakistan and Iraq. They believe that one day the final successor to Ali, called the **Mahdi**, will come to set up the perfect Muslim state.

Ali

Ali ibn Abi Talib (598–661) was Muhammad's cousin. When his father died, Ali was taken in by Muhammad and raised almost as his son. When Muhammad died, many people, including his daughter Fatima, wanted Ali to be the caliph. But the Muslims chose Abu Bakr as the first caliph.

Ali became the fourth caliph. But other Muslims supported Muawiya, the governor of Damascus, and this started the split between the Sunni and Shi'ite Muslims. Ali was mortally wounded by an attacker in the mosque at Kufa. It was three days before he died, insisting all the time that his attacker should not be tortured. Ali's shrine at Najaf, in Iraq, is still a place of pilgrimage for Shi'ites today.

D SOURCE

Sayings of Ali:

- If you love Allah, reject your heart's love of the world.
- One who is proud of worldly possessions in life is ignorant.

E SOURCE

I have come to you with the authority of God to rule you. It is your duty to obey me in what I think is best. It is your right that I should be fair. If you see me managing your affairs well, respond to me well.

Muawiya, quoted in 'The Majesty that was Islam' by W. Montgomery Watt, 1974.

C SOURCE

A Shi'ite mosque, near Baghdad in present-day Iraq. It was built in the 16th century.

3.1 The Umayyads

Even before Ali died, Muawiya claimed to be the true caliph. His family, the **Umayyads**, provided the next fourteen caliphs. They ruled until 750. Muawiya moved the capital of Islam from the holy city of Medina to **Damascus,** capital of **Syria.** He had been governor of Syria for Uthman. His supporters and his army were there. Each Umayyad caliph named a relative to be his successor before he died. This was to avoid arguments. But it meant that a ruling family was being created.

The Umayyads ruled well for a while. Under them, Arab rule grew to the borders of modern-day France in the west and India in the east. They built fabulous mosques like the **Dome of the Rock** in Jerusalem (see page 7). They allowed their people to bring their problems to them and consulted advisers about their policies. They were just like the Arab sheiks of the desert. They kept many of the efficient Christian clerks of the Byzantine Empire, but put Arabs in the top jobs. They had a postal system using riders on horseback to reach all parts of their lands. Arabic replaced Greek and Persian as the language of the captured territory. They started the first Arab coinage, the gold **dinar** and the silver **dirham.** Before this, the Arabs had used the coins of other countries. All of this meant the Umayyads had firmer control than any caliphs before.

But they started to neglect the rules of Islam. They did not base their laws on the Koran. They were not good Muslims like earlier caliphs. They built lavish palaces outside the towns, where they spent their time hunting or drinking and dancing, surrounded by beautiful women, poets and musicians. Their subjects became unhappy with the Umayyads.
Many Muslims, especially the Shi'ites, thought that the beliefs

A SOURCE

The court is paved with white marble. The walls of the mosque are faced with multi-coloured marble and above this are mosaics of gold and other colours, showing figures of trees and towns and beautiful inscriptions. Every well known tree and town can be found on these walls. The capitals of the columns are covered with gold, and the vaulting above is decorated with mosaic in arabesque designs.

A 10th century visitor describing the court of the Great Mosque at Damascus, built between 705 and 715.

C SOURCE

Handsome and enormously strong, a poet and musician, Walid II led the good life at his palace at Mshatta, where he filled his swimming pool with wine, and missed public prayers when he was not in a mood, or a condition, to appear. He was murdered in 744.

From 'The Splendors of Islam' by Wilfrid Blunt, 1976.

of Islam were being forgotten. The Christians and Jews under Arab control became restless too. They didn't like having to pay more taxes than Muslims. The Persians were also restless. They had a glorious history and didn't like the way the Arabs looked down upon them. The bedouin soldiers, who had fought for the land the Umayyads ruled, began to settle down and live as farmers. Many of them didn't want to fight for the Umayyads any longer.

A group of Arabs began to use this discontent to stir up trouble against the Umayyads. They had settled in the lands captured from the Persian Empire but they were Arab descendants of one of Muhammad's uncles, al-Abbas. They called themselves the **Abbasids.** They started a propaganda campaign against the Umayyads. Then they raised an army from their supporters. At the **Battle of the Great Zab** in 750, they defeated and killed the caliph. Umayyad control of Islam thus ended.

Mosaics, pictures made up of tiny pieces of tile, around the arches and columns of the Great Mosque at Damascus, 715.

al-Walid II

Caliph al-Walid II (708–44) was the Umayyad caliph from 743 to 744. His brief caliphate shows how far some caliphs fell below the example of Muhammad. He succeeded his uncle, Hisham, who was a very religious man. Walid quickly became notorious for his extravagant lifestyle. He moved from one desert palace to another, spending a fortune on buildings, poets and wine. Wine is against Islamic law. One story claims that he dived into a pool of wine and drank himself unconscious.

Walid commanded no respect or loyalty. His empire was in tatters. His family had him murdered. In 744, three more caliphs came and went, and the Umayyad dynasty was overthrown in 750.

D

SOURCE

3.2 Early Islamic Art

Before Muhammad, the Arabs were mostly nomadic farmers or traders. They had little art of their own. But as Arab rule expanded, they settled down among Greeks and Syrians in the north, Persians in the east and Egyptians and Berbers in the west. They therefore 'discovered' the art of all these people. As they built their new towns, mosques and palaces, they used the best local craftsmen to help them. But the Arabs didn't just take the art of other people. They influenced the work they had done. So a new, typically Islamic, style of art arose. It can be seen in the years 600–1000 all around the Muslim world – local styles with a clear Arab influence.

For example, the Arabs learned about **mosaics** from the Byzantines. These are pictures on walls or floors made of small pieces of tile, stone or glass. The Dome of the Rock in Jerusalem and the Great Mosque in Damascus have large mosaics. Following Arab tastes, scenes from nature are common. But so are shapes and **patterns**. The Arabs liked work in **stucco**, fine plaster to decorate walls and columns. Patterns can also be seen in **window grills**, carved from stone or marble or made of metal. Early Muslims also made patterns on gold and silver and on ornaments carved from ivory, wood and rock crystal. The most famous pattern is called **arabesque** (a design of flowing lines, often with leaves and flowers). There were probably many **wall paintings** in the Umayyad mosques and palaces. But there is a problem with these. Many early mosques and palaces were made from brick, not stone. Brick is soft and does not last well. Some buildings were also destroyed later by invaders.

The Arabs also developed new ways of decorating **pottery**. One was a new shiny look called **lustreware**, which was also used on **tiles**. There were also splendid **carpets**, sometimes woven from silk. But no carpets survive from this period. Everyday articles such as pots and carpets were used and thrown away by their owners. They didn't make an effort to save them for us!

Early Arabic writing, known as **Kufic**, looks very simple. But the Koran was written in Arabic. So Muslims developed more and more attractive forms of writing, until it became an art form. This art of beautiful writing is called **calligraphy** and can be seen on Islamic books, paintings, pottery, mosaics and carpets. It is the most common feature of Islamic art.

A

A bowl decorated with kufic script, made in eastern Iran in the 10th century. The inscription says, 'Generosity is characteristic of the people of paradise'.

B

An ivory casket from Spain made in about 1050. It is typical of Muslim work and has calligraphic decoration round the rim.

Tile decorations from the Dome of the Rock mosque, Jerusalem, built in the 7th century.

A mosaic floor from the bath of an Umayyad palace built in about 740.

A 10th century dish made in eastern Iran. The pattern was made by painting the design and then covering it with a transparent glaze.

al-Malik

Caliph Abd al-Malik (about 646–705) was the fifth Umayyad caliph. His caliphate, 685–705, was mostly a period of calm and progress. He was the first caliph to insist on the use of Arabic throughout his empire. He introduced the very first Arab coins, the gold dinar and the silver dirham.

Al-Malik ordered the construction of the Dome of the Rock (see page 7). This magnificent shrine commemorates two great events. The first is the willingness of Abraham to sacrifice to God his son Isaac. But the Dome, known to Arabs as Qubbat as-Sakrah, is also built around the rock from which Muhammad is said to have visited Heaven, travelling there and back on his white stallion.

The Dome of the Rock is an octagonal building. Its walls and dome were originally covered with mosaics of glass and gold, though its appearance has changed much since it was first built.

3.3 The Abbasids

We saw in Unit 3.1 how the **Umayyads**, who ruled the Islamic world from Damascus until 750, were overthrown by the Abbasids. But more changed than just the ruling family.

The **Abbasids** were Arabs who were descended from Muhammad's family. But they had settled in the area captured from the Persian Empire and intermarried with Persians. They adopted Persian customs and employed Persian officials. They shut themselves away behind the walls of their palaces and lived lives of glorious luxury, like the old Persian kings. They even started to claim holy status, calling themselves 'The Shadow of God on Earth'. Even Muhammad had not gone this far. The 'rightly-guided' caliphs had mixed with their people and lived fairly ordinary lives. The Umayyads had consulted with other Arab sheiks and taken advice from them. The old Arab ways were changing.

The Abbasids also built a new capital at **Baghdad**. It became a centre for world trade. Ships came to Baghdad along the River Tigris or the River Euphrates:
- from China, bringing silk, ink and peacocks,
- from India with rubies, silver, ebony and dyes,
- from Egypt with grain and glass,
- from Africa with slaves and gold,
- from Spain with leather,
- from Russia with furs.

The Muslim traders also brought back knowledge, ideas and skills from the countries they visited. For example, the Arabs learned how to make paper from the Chinese in about 750. The Islamic world became a mixture of cultures: Arab, Persian and others from all over the world. The early years of the Abbasid era were the richest period of Islamic history.

The Abbasid dynasty at Baghdad lasted 500 years, until 1258. Many things changed in the Islamic world during this time and we shall see in later units how the Abbasids lost control of their lands. But some things did not change. The borders of Islam stayed the same, stretching from India and China in the east to the Atlantic Ocean in the west. Arabic remained the common language and laws were still based on the Koran. Islam, founded by the Arabs, remained unchallenged as the religion.

A **SOURCE**

This dynasty ruled with a policy of mixed religion and kingship. The best and most religious of men obeyed them out of religion, and the remainder obeyed them out of fear.

An Arab historian, quoted by Desmond Stewart in 'Early Islam', 1967.

B **SOURCE**

The caliph himself was unavailable to all but a privileged few, who had to make their way past many guards and officials to get to him.

From 'Early Islam' by Desmond Stewart, 1967.

SOURCE C

Caliph Abu Jafar adopted the name of al-Mansur. It means 'the one helped to victory by God' and was chosen to make it seem that the ruler was supported by God. Harun's title was al-Rashid, 'the rightly-guided'.

From 'The Majesty that was Islam' by W. Montgomery Watt, 1974.

SOURCE D

Consider Caliph Harun's titles : 'The Holy, the Just, the High-Born, the Omnipotent; the Gardener of the Vale of Islam, the Lion of the Impassable Forests, the Rider of the Spotless Horse, the Cypress on the Golden Hill, the Master of Spears, the Shadow of God on Earth, the Commander of the Faithful... The Caliph!'

From 'Iraq, Land of Two Rivers' by Gavin Young, 1980.

al-Mansur

Caliph al-Mansur (about 709–75) was the second Abbasid caliph, from 754–75. At first, he lived in his homeland at Kufa in Persia. In 762, he made Baghdad the new capital. Its design shows how unsafe the Abbasids felt. The city was surrounded by two strong walls. Only the caliph, his officials and soldiers lived inside them. Other people lived outside, crowded between the tributaries of the River Tigris.

SOURCE E

A miniature painting dated 1237. It shows the caliph's standard bearers announcing his arrival.

3.4 Baghdad

Abu Jafar al-Mansur, the second Abbasid caliph, built a new capital in 762. He chose a trading village called **Baghdad**. It was on the banks of the River Tigris and linked to the River Euphrates by canal. It took four years to build. Under the caliph **Harun al-Rashid** (786–809), it was the most splendid city in the world. We have Arabic manuscripts and travellers' accounts which describe it. Baghdad had 1.5 million people, measured five miles across and had hundreds of mosques and over 65,000 public baths. It had gardens, racetracks and pavilions. Many people who lived there gave up some of their Arab ways of the desert, using mattresses and tables, adopting porcelain from the Chinese, and developing the games of polo, backgammon and chess from the East.

Poetry and literature also blossomed in Baghdad. The book *Tales of the Arabian Nights* dates from this time. It is a collection of stories from all over the world. Some are set in Baghdad and feature Harun and his family. These include the stories of Aladin, Ali Baba, Sinbad the Sailor and the beautiful princess Scheherazade. They paint a fairy-story world of dashing Arab princes riding pure white horses through a city of bustling market places and sparkling minarets. It is a picture repeated in countless films. It is based on the truth, but it gives us a distorted view of what things were really like.

B SOURCE

I slipped back into my dream as we flew into Iraq, a dream of Baghdad formed by two old Hollywood movies, *The Thief of Baghdad*, and *A Thousand and One Nights*. In it, I float in a gleaming technicolour city of towering walls and arched gates, golden domes and minarets like sticks of candy. Harun al-Rashid, surrounded by slaves bearing scimitars, sits there and a beautiful girl in see-through Oriental trousers belly-dances to the sound of tambourines, flutes, harps and – strangely – jazz saxophones.

From 'Iraq, Land of Two Rivers' by Gavin Young, 1980.

A SOURCE

Baghdad was built in the form of a circle nearly two miles across with a deep moat surrounding three huge, sloping walls. Of these, the middle one was the largest, some 112 feet in height, 164 feet wide at the base and 46 feet across the top. It was fortified with look-out towers. The round city was cut into four wedge-shaped parts by two highways which cut across it at right angles, with gates through each of the walls. The space between the middle and outer walls was left clear for defence. Between the middle and inner walls were the houses of the courtiers and army officers. Behind the inner wall lived the caliph's relatives and the most important officials. The hub of the city was the caliph's palace. Between the inner and middle walls each of the main streets became lined with all manner of shops, making four central markets. The ordinary people of Baghdad lived outside the walls.

From 'Early Islam' by Desmond Stewart, 1967.

al-Rashid

Harun al-Rashid (about 764–809) is the most famous of the Abbasid caliphs. He won the caliphate in 786 after a war against his brother Musa al-Hadi which ended when al-Hadi died in mysterious circumstances. From this unpromising start came a splendid reign. Harun sent ambassadors to the courts of Charlemagne in the west and the Chinese Emperor in the east. A sign of his wealth is that he had a personal collection of 1000 jewelled rings at his death.

Nothing now remains of the Abbasid capital of Baghdad. Because there were no local sources of stone, it was built from clay bricks dried in the sun. Unfortunately brick does not last as well as stone. Invaders flattened much of the city and modern Baghdad is built on the ruins. However, remains of other Abbasid buildings have survived at **Samarra**. This was a city built 80 miles along the Tigris from Baghdad. It was briefly the Abbasid capital from 833 to 893. Samarra has the largest mosque ever built, the **Great Mosque**, with its spiral minaret, or **Malawiya**. Samarra gives us a hint of the glories of Baghdad under the Abbasids.

D

SOURCE

C

SOURCE

An image of the city of Baghdad from a Hollywood film.

The spiral minaret, or Malawiya, at Samarra.

3.5 The Role of Men and Women

The Koran said that men and women should be equal. But it also said that they should have different roles. (See Sources A and B.)

In some ways, the rules of Islam brought few changes and Muslims continued to live as they had before. Women stayed in charge of the home and the children. Men provided food and shelter. Men continued to have more than one wife if they wanted. Arranged marriages were common. This was a system where a marriage was arranged by the families of young Muslims. Usually, they didn't make the choice themselves. This was also common in many other parts of the world. (See Source D.)

But in other ways, Islam improved the lives of women. There had been rules to protect women before. But Muslim men were more likely to follow the rules when they were in the Koran. The Koran said that all women should be protected; that men should behave properly towards them; that they should be respected.

SOURCE A

In Islam women have the same rights to own property and be educated. The Koran requires men and women to behave modestly and decently towards one another. For example, men should always be covered from the navel to the knees. Women should cover their whole bodies except their hands and face.

From 'The Muslim World' by Richard Tames, 1982.

SOURCE B

Women are not subservient to men in Muslim society. The man is responsible for the family's welfare and business outside the home, and the woman controls things inside. But women expect to be treated with respect. They regard themselves as equally important as men; this was made clear in the Koran.

From 'Islam' by Rosalyn Kendrick, 1989.

SOURCE C

The arrangements were started by the mothers. Then a contract was drawn up, stating the girl's age (usually 12–20), and the price that the man paid to his bride, which remained hers even if they were divorced. Should a man and wife argue, they could appeal to a qadi, or judge, who could settle domestic disputes. If the qadi's decision failed to solve the problem, the husband could divorce his wife. He could remarry immediately but his wife had to wait three months. (This was in case she was pregnant.)

From 'Early Islam' by Desmond Stewart, 1967, describing Islamic arrangements as they would have been in about 1300.

SOURCE D

Parents often chose their child's partner. This was partly because parents paid a dowry, or money to start the marriage. It was usual to give the potential husband and wife a chance to meet, and to refuse at least one suggested partner. The idea of marrying for love was seen as foolish. The idea was that a couple should grow fond of each other after marriage.

From 'Skills in History' by P. Shuter, J. Child and D. Taylor, 1989, describing arrangements made by Christians in England in about 1600.

The Koran allowed men to have up to four wives as long as they treated them all equally. Having more than one marriage partner is called **polygamy**. Muslim women could only have one husband. There are many possible reasons for polygamy. Muslims believe that in the Koran, God said that marriage is the religious duty and privilege of **all** women. Allowing men to have more than one wife meant that there would always be enough men for all women to be able to marry. It is interesting that permission for polygamy was revealed to Muhammad just after many Muslim men were killed in the Battle of Uhud. Muslims also say that polygamy means that men are less likely to be unfaithful to their wives, and that this reduces the likelihood of unmarried mothers. They also say that some women welcome the extra help with housework and looking after children, especially if they are ill for a long time.

SOURCE E

The housework didn't allow a Muslim wife to keep her feminine charms. The old Arab custom of having young wives living with older house-proud ladies was worth keeping. So Muhammad came up with an answer. Muslims might have up to four wives at a time.

From 'The Clash of Cultures' by Brian Catchpole, 1981.

Ayesha

Ayesha (about 614–78) was one of Muhammad's fourteen wives. She was a daughter of Abu Bakr, his closest friend, who was the first caliph. Ayesha married Muhammad when she was about eight years old, but did not live with him until she was twelve.

Ayesha became one of the most famous women in Muslim history. Despite Muhammad's position, she did all of the housework. She kept Muhammad company even when he stayed awake all night at prayer. She became an expert on Islamic laws, particularly on matters concerning women. She was once accused of being unfaithful to Muhammad, but he received a revelation that she was innocent.

SOURCE F

A qadi listening to a dispute between a man and his wives, (painting dated 1237).

3.6 Religious Life

The religious rules of Islam have remained the same since the death of Muhammad. For example, the key beliefs were, and still are, the '**Five Pillars of Islam**': faith, prayer, charity, fasting and pilgrimage.

The first pillar was faith in Allah and His teaching. All that was needed to become a Muslim was to believe and say, 'There is no god but Allah, and Muhammad is His Prophet'. This chant is called the **shahada** and it is still used at a Muslim's birth, throughout life and at funerals. It is a poetic phrase when spoken in Arabic: 'La ilaha illa Allah; Muhammad rasul Allah'. Muslims also believed that the Koran was the exact words of God. God made the world and would send people to Heaven or Hell when they died. They believed that Jesus was also an important prophet of God, but not his son.

The second pillar, called **salat**, was prayer five times a day. Before each prayer, Muslims washed their face, arms and feet and passed their wet hands over their heads. Muslims were called to prayer at the mosques by **muezzins** shouting from the minarets. Prayers were not led by priests, but by laymen called **imams**. Because the prayers had to be said in the direction of the Ka'ba in Mecca, a decorated arch, or **mihrab**, was always set in the wall of the mosque to show this direction.

A Muslim's funeral followed a strict ritual which included the wailing of women and readings from the Koran. Washed and wrapped in a seamless white shroud, (dipped on pilgrimage in the waters of Mecca's sacred Zamzam well), the body was laid to rest on its side, facing the holy city.

From 'Early Islam' by Desmond Stewart, 1967.

A group of Muslim pilgrims from a painting dated 1237.

The next pillar was **zakat**. This said that all Muslims should give part of their income to charity every year. The fourth pillar, called **saum**, was fasting (going without food) during the Muslim month of **Ramadan**. This is when the Koran was first revealed to Muhammad. The final pillar was the **hajj**, the promise to go on a pilgrimage to Mecca at least once. A trip to the Ka'ba had been an Arab tradition before Muhammad and Islam adopted it.

Muslims also made laws based on their religion. These laws are called the **shari'a**. They make up most of the laws of Muslim countries. They are based on the Koran and **Hadith**. Hadith are the wise sayings of Muhammad. They were told over and over again until eventually they were written down.

Muslims also promised to fight for Islam if it was threatened. A holy war to defend Islam is sometimes called a **jihad**, but this also means any other kind of effort for Islam. Muslims were not allowed to eat pork, drink alcohol, gamble or lend money for interest.

Jalal ud-din Rumi

Jalal ud-din Rumi (1207–73) is the most famous of Muslim sufis. A sufi is a religious leader who has a very close relationship with God and spends much time in prayer and contemplation. Jalal ud-din Rumi began having visions from the age of six. He taught that Muslims should be ashamed to ask for anything in prayer; they should be content. This-was true submission, true Islam.

Jalal ud-din Rumi also founded the whirling dervishes. This is an order of sufis famous for their sacred dance. Dressed in white robes, they start gliding and spinning which helps the dancers enter a trance-like state and gain closer contact with God.

C

SOURCE

A Muslim burial. The men are wearing thin black strips of mourning on their heads. The domes in the background are the tops of the tombs of wealthy Muslims (picture dated 1237).

3.7 Islamic Medicine

The Arabs were keen to learn from the people they conquered. Caliph Mamun, caliph from 813 to 833, built a **House of Wisdom** in Baghdad. Muslim scholars worked there, translating books about medicine, mathematics and science. They searched for books as far away as India and Africa.

Medicine

At the time of Muhammad, many Arabs believed that illness was caused by the gods. But when they conquered Syria and Persia, they found books with better ideas. These had been written by Ancient Greek scholars, like Galen and Hippocrates. They translated these books into Arabic.

Muslim scholars also went further. Hippocrates had stressed the need to observe the patient very carefully when studying disease. **Rhazes**, a Persian born in 865, used this method. He studied patients with fever and learned to tell the difference between measles and smallpox. He wrote over 100 books on medicine. Another Persian, **Avicenna**, born in 980, wrote the *Canon of Medicine*, a survey of the treatment of all known diseases. It was used by doctors in Europe as a textbook until the 17th century.

Muslim doctors used a variety of **drugs**. Potions were made from animal and plant extracts and chemicals like copper sulphate. In Baghdad, inspectors called to check the quality of the drugs. A chemist caught cheating his customers could be fined or even beaten.

By 850 Baghdad had its own hospital. Soon there were 34 hospitals in the Muslim world, more than in all of Europe. Some hospitals had separate wards for different illnesses and special areas for the insane. There were clinics for outpatients and doctors travelled to the areas outside large towns. From 931 doctors in Baghdad had to pass examinations to get a licence.

From Rhazes, 'On Smallpox and Measles'. Dated about 900 .

A page from the Arabic translation of a book by Dioscorides, a Greek doctor. Detailed records of plants used to make medicines were kept. Dated about 1229.

B

SOURCE

Rhazes

Abu-Bakr Muhammad ibn-Zakariya al-Razi (865–923), known as Rhazes, was the greatest doctor of his age. He studied chemistry in Baghdad and discovered ammonia. He collected Greek, Syrian and Arab books about medicine. He studied these, added his own discoveries, and recorded his findings. He made studies of kidneys and gallstones, explained smallpox and German measles, and exposed some of Galen's errors (a famous doctor in ancient Greece). His 25 volume *Al-Hawi* was written out by his pupils after his death. It was translated into Latin in 1282 and printed in 1486. Western doctors used his medical practices well into the 16th century.

C **SOURCE**

They took me to see a knight who had a boil on his leg and a woman with tuberculosis. I applied a poultice to the leg and the boil began to heal. I ordered a fresh diet for the woman. Then a French doctor came and said, "This man has no idea how to cure these people". He sent for a strong man and an axe. The doctor put the leg on a block of wood and said, "Strike a mighty blow and cut cleanly". The marrow spurted out and the patient died at once. He examined the woman and said, "The devil has got into her brain". He took a razor, removed the brain and rubbed it with salt. The woman died at once.

A Muslim doctor describing European medical treatment during the Crusades. Dated about 1150.

Surgery was also improved. **Abulcasis**, a Muslim born in Spain in 936, translated the ideas of the Greek, Paul of Aegina. Muslim doctors practised his methods and improved them. They operated on eyes to remove cataracts and removed cancers. They used tubes as stomach drains to remove fluids and they could amputate arms and legs. They used opium to make patients sleep when they were in pain.

Traders and soldiers who visited Muslim lands took some of this knowledge back to Europe. Most European scholars read Latin and did not know the books of the Ancient Greeks. The first school of medicine in Europe was set up at Salerno in Italy by soldiers coming home from the Crusades. (The Crusades were battles between the Muslims and Christians.)

A medieval Muslim doctor with a patient.

D **SOURCE**

3.8 Mathematics and Science

On their travels, the Arabs learned a new system of **numbers**. Until then, most people used Roman numbers to count things, (I, II, III, IV, V, etc.). But this was not a good system. The Hindus in India were using a better system (1, 2, 3, 4, 5, etc.). The Arabs copied this. It became so well known that we still use it today. But they didn't just copy, they also developed new theories in algebra and geometry. Better mathematics helped farmers measure the size of a field, traders know the storage area of a ship or builders work out the strength of arches.

Muslim scientists also copied useful ideas. For example, they found out about labour-saving devices like the **windmill** and **wheelbarrows** from the Chinese. This is also where they learned how to make **paper**. But they also discovered things themselves. Trying to make new drugs for doctors, they learned about chemicals. (The word *chemistry* comes from Arabic.) By chance, this showed them how to make steel for swords and dyes for carpetmakers. Also, at this time no one knew how eyes worked. Some people believed that they sent out invisible rays. But **Alhazen**, a Persian scientist, discovered that the eye sees light from the sun reflecting off things around us. This started **optics**, the science of light. Later, it helped people make telescopes and microscopes.

The study of the stars, or **astronomy**, was a favourite science of the Arabs. In the desert, travellers needed the stars for direction at night. Muslims also needed to know the time and the direction of Mecca for their daily prayers. To help them learn more about the stars, caliph Harun al-Rashid had the ideas of Ptolemy, the Ancient Greek scholar, translated into Arabic. Caliph Mamun built an observatory to study the stars at the House of Wisdom. The Muslims also improved the Greek device called the **astrolabe**. This was an instrument which could be used to measure the height and position of the stars and to tell the time.

A SOURCE

An Arab called Jazari invented this machine in about 1250. Machines like this were used in Iraq. The donkey moved a post which was connected to wheels with gears on them; these wheels lifted four large scoops which can just be seen under the water on the diagram. The scoops rose one at a time, lifting water from the river into canals that watered the fields. This was a big help to farmers.

B SOURCE

A picture from a 16th century Muslim manuscript showing astronomers studying the stars.

This is the same simple sum in Roman and Arabic numerals. The Roman numerals are very hard to add up. The Romans had no symbol for zero and you can't separate their numbers into columns of tens and units.

$$\begin{array}{r} XIII \\ + \ VI \\ \hline XIX \end{array} \qquad \begin{array}{r} 13 \\ + \ 6 \\ \hline 19 \end{array}$$

An Arab map of the constellation of the Great Bear. How were maps like these useful?

al-Khwarizmi

Muhammad ibn-Musa al-Khwarizmi (?–about 844) was a Muslim mathematician. Little is known about his life, although some of his writings have survived. He was a Persian who wrote in Arabic and worked for Caliph al-Mamum in Baghdad.

Al-Khwarizmi wrote the first astronomical tables and the first written work on arithmetic, containing the calculation of square roots. He introduced Hindu numerals into the Muslim world. He is famous for his book, *Hisab al-Jabr w-al-Muqabalah* (*The Calculation of Integration and Equation*). This work, known as *al-Jabr* for short, is the basis of algebra, and was far in advance of Western scholarship.

raders and travellers were also helped by the astrolabe. It ould be used with maps of the stars to find exactly where avellers were and the direction they needed to go. The Arabs uld now find out about countries thousands of miles away. hey visited central Africa with its mysterious animals. The rst Arab description of China appeared in 851. Muslims isited Russia in 921. In the 11th century the scientist **Biruni** isited India. His detailed book told the whole story, including ined-together twins he had seen in Siam (hence 'Siamese twins'). Arab geographers drew maps of the world. They became convinced that the world was round.

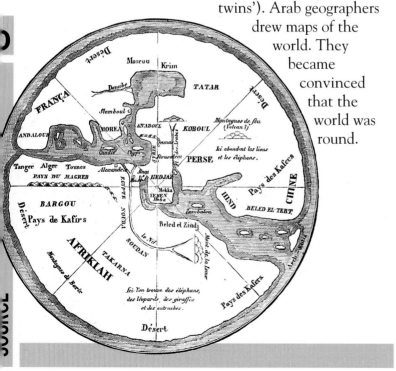

This is a French copy of an old Arab map. How can you tell it was a Muslim map?

3.9 Schools and Universities

Before Muhammad, there were no schools for Arab children. Parents taught their children what they needed for life in the desert. Education was important to Muhammad. His sayings make this clear. Teaching the Koran was vital. The first thing a father taught his children was the shahada. (See page 28.) Another thing was to make sure the Muslims had a strong army. Caliph Umar told Muslims, 'Teach your boys swimming, archery, horse-riding and the appreciation of poetry'.

As soon as the Muslims settled down in the lands they had conquered they started to set up schools. Rich parents had private teachers for their children. But the mosques soon set up schools called **kuttabs**, which charged very low fees. Boys of seven and over would go. Most of the time they chanted or wrote from the Koran. But there was also a little poetry and mathematics. Girls might be sent along for the teaching about Islam but that was probably all.

For the children of the poor, this was as much teaching as they got. But the Arabs needed clerks and administrators, and by about 700 the kuttabs were expanding and taking older children for parents who could afford the fees. The Koran remained the most important part of their education, although mathematics was also important.

A scene from a mosque school in Baghdad in 1237. One boy in the background swings the fan to keep the class cool. Another stands to chant the Koran. The others, all boys, scratch the Koran on to stone tablets.

B

SOURCE

A scene from the library of a mosque, also dated 1237. Young men listen while one of them reads from a book – not necessarily the Koran. Notice all the books on the shelves.

There was no system of higher education for many years. Only the sons of the very rich continued their studies in their teenage years. They had specially qualified teachers. But there were discussion groups for adults in philosophy, mathematics and poetry at the mosques. The mosques also often had their own libraries which people could use.

Then in 978, in Cairo, Egypt, the al-Azhar mosque was founded. Its school grew into a university. It is perhaps the oldest in the world. It had free tuition, plus board and lodging. Later other Muslim universities were founded at Baghdad, Granada in Spain, and Fez in Morocco. These were all started long before the first chartered university in Christian Europe. That was set up with the help of Muslims at Naples in Italy just before Oxford and Cambridge universities in England.

D Every mosque has a school where young Muslims do their Islamic studies. In Britain this usually takes place between 4 and 6 p.m., five nights a week.

Children in Muslim countries do their Islamic studies in normal school lessons during the day. They are the most important lessons but there are lots of other subjects.

Boys and girls start Islamic studies aged five. Girls finish at 12; boys go on until they are at least 15.

A description of Muslim education today from 'Islam' by Rosalyn Kendrick, 1989.

al-Mu'izz

Al-Mu'izz (931–75) was the Fatimid ruler who founded the al-Azhar university in Cairo. The Fatimids were a family who claimed descent from Fatima, the daughter of Muhammad. From 909, they began to take control of North Africa. In 969, al-Mu'izz's general, Jawhar, captured Egypt. The Fatimids were Shi'ite Muslims, and, surrounded by Sunnis, they built a new, strongly fortified capital called al-Qahira, known in the West as Cairo.

But the Fatimids were also keen to encourage learning. In 970, al-Mu'izz ordered the building of a mosque at Cairo, with its own school and library. This mosque, the al-Azhar ('The Splendid'), soon grew into a university. It is considered by some to be the oldest university in the world. It still exists as a thriving university with two major campuses in Cairo and four in other major Egyptian towns.

3.10 Trade and Ships

Baghdad was ideally sited for trade. It was on a canal linking the Rivers Tigris and Euphrates and close to the Mediterranean and Red Seas. From about 800 its **bazaars** (market places) were bustling with traders from all over the known world. They bought and sold with the silver **dirham** or the gold **dinar**. Money-changers would swap other coins for these. Later they took written promises to pay which were like cheques (the word comes from the Arabic *sakk*).

Some of the traders went by **land**. Traders going north into Russia and Scandinavia used horses and carts. They took perfume, carpets, grain from the fields around Baghdad and rice from Egypt, and came back with furs, falcons and armour. The Arabs used camels to carry heavy loads over long distances. From about 900, they were crossing the Sahara into central Africa. They took leather, glass and pottery, and came back with black slaves, gold, ostrich feathers and ivory. The long journeys across hot, dry deserts were hard, thirsty and very dangerous. Bandits raided the trading caravans.

Muslim leaders set up strings of small fortresses, called **caravansaries**, in the deserts where traders could rest overnight. Otherwise they slept under the stars before setting off again at a steady three miles per hour on their long journey.

SOURCE A

A market scene in Baghdad in 1237. A Muslim family look at the black slaves on sale. The trader in the background weighs coins to be sure of their value.

SOURCE B

A hoard of silver from a 10th century Viking grave containing Arab coins, found in Sweden.

A map of North Africa dated about 1400. It would have been drawn from the accounts of Arab travellers and shows an Arab trader being offered a gold nugget by the King of Mali. Many of the main settlements are shown by mosques.

Other trade went by **sea**. The Arabs had no tradition of sailing but they quickly learned new skills. They sailed across the Mediterranean to Italy and Spain. They also had fast **dhows** which sailed down the Red Sea or the Persian Gulf to the Indian Ocean. They brought back silk, peacocks, paper and porcelain from China and rubies, spices and dyes from India and East Africa.

From about 1200 they went even further, bringing back pepper, nutmeg, cinnamon and cloves from Indonesia and the Philippines. Muslim sailors used the **astrolabe**, borrowed from the Ancient Greeks, to find their position and the magnetic **compass**, discovered in China, for direction. They also invented a new way of arranging the ship's sails. Ships usually had 'square rigging', square sails *across* the ships, which need wind from behind to blow them along. The Muslims developed **'lateen'** sails, which were rigged *along* the ships, allowing them to sail into the wind. This made ships easier to manoeuvre and allowed them to sail along rivers to the cities.

There were practically no Europeans trading with Africa and the Far East at this time. Europe depended on the Arabs for all of their goods and knowledge from these far-off places. The voyages of sailors like Christopher Columbus would not have been possible without the instruments and sails which Europe learned about from the Muslims.

Mansa Musa

Mansa Musa (?–about 1337) was the King of Mali in Africa from 1312 to about 1337. He was a devout Muslim and spread Islam as he expanded his control over most of western Africa.

Arab traders sailed around the coasts of Africa and sent caravans across the Sahara Desert. They traded in jewels and precious metals with Mali's rich cities of Timbuktu and Gao. This trade made Mansa Musa so wealthy that when he went on a pilgrimage to Mecca in 1324, he took with him 500 slaves and 100 camels bearing gold and gifts, escorted by 15,000 cavalry. He returned with many scholars who started a university at Timbuktu, and with Sahali, a Spanish architect who built mosques in his kingdom.

3.11 The End of the Abbasids

The Abbasids ruled the Islamic world from 750. They were the official caliphs until 1258. However, they lost *real* control long before this. First they lost control of the distant provinces. For example, they never gained control of the Muslim rulers of **Spain** and they soon lost control of **Egypt**. Then, even in **Baghdad**, they ended up taking orders from other people.

Events in Spain

Muslim soldiers invaded Spain in 711. Their armies entered France and got to within 200 miles of the English Channel. But in 732 they were defeated at the **Battle of Poitiers**, near Tours, by Charles Martel, king of the Franks. Even so, Muslims ruled parts of Spain until 1492. The Muslims in Spain were known as **Moors**. They were never controlled from Baghdad.

First one Muslim family and then another ruled Spain. A series of important towns grew up. At first, the main one was **Cordoba**. Others were **Toledo**, **Seville** and **Granada**. They were the most splendid towns in Europe at the time. In the 13th century the Moors built the famous **Alhambra Palace** in Granada. In some bedrooms it even had flushing toilets, made possible by diverting a whole river under the palace. Traders from all over Europe came to buy goods from the Moors. It was in Spain that Europeans first gained the knowledge and skills of the Muslim world. Europe learned about Arabic numbers, papermaking, medical knowledge and musical instruments like the guitar. Spain still shows signs of Muslim culture in its buildings, its music and its food.

B SOURCE

In the ninth and tenth centuries, Cordoba was a city of 200,000 houses, 600 mosques and 900 public baths. Its streets were paved and water was piped to the people. Its library had 600,000 books and there were 50 other libraries in the region. Primary schools were common. In agriculture, the Moors introduced new crops, notably figs, dates, rice and cotton. They improved animal rearing and irrigation of the fields. The Moors had the biggest trading fleet in the Mediterranean and expanded the mining, wool and silk industries.

From 'Spain' by Hugh Thomas, 1964.

Although it is not the most attractive building the Moors left in Spain, this is an interesting one. It was a hotel for traders, built in Granada in about 1350.

A SOURCE

Events in Egypt

By 850, the Abbasids were too weak to control their provinces. In 868 **Ibn Tulun**, their governor in Egypt, refused to pay their taxes and began to rule by himself. He had a large Turkish army to keep him in power. After Ibn Tulun died, the **Fatimids** invaded Egypt from North Africa. They were Shi'ites who claimed to be descended from Muhammad's daughter Fatima. They turned the city of **Cairo** into their new capital. The other major town of Fatimid Egypt was **Fustat**, which had half a million people, some living in five storey buildings with running water and sewers. In 1171 the Fatimids were overthrown by a group of Sunni Muslims from eastern Turkey led by Salah ad-Din. In the West we call him **Saladin**. He set up a ruling Turkish family in Egypt known as the **Ayyubids**. They relied upon Turkish slaves to form a huge army which kept them in power. But in 1250 these slaves, known as **Mamlukes**, rebelled. The Mamlukes ruled Egypt until 1517. Through all this upheaval, Egypt prospered. It had huge food surpluses to sell and Cairo was the wealthiest trading city in the Mediterranean in the 12th century. Its famous al-Azhar university is the oldest still existing in the world.

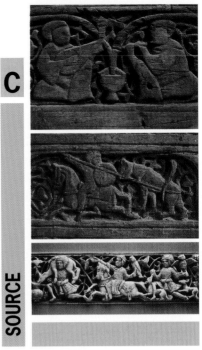

Carvings from the Fatimid period in Egypt. The top two are wooden panellings from walls: one was in a palace, the other in a hospital. The bottom one was an ivory decoration on furniture.

The decline of the Abbasids

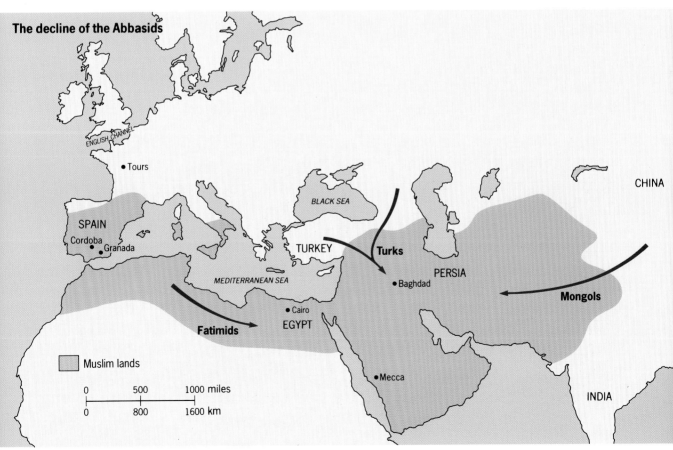

CHINA

ENGLISH CHANNEL

• Tours

BLACK SEA

SPAIN

Cordoba
• • Granada

TURKEY

Turks

PERSIA

MEDITERRANEAN SEA

• Baghdad

• Cairo

Mongols

Fatimids

EGYPT

Muslim lands

0	500	1000 miles
0	800	1600 km

• Mecca

INDIA

Events in Baghdad

The Abbasids had taken over control of the Muslim world in 750. But by about 850 the Arab caliphs were chosen by the army and had to do what the soldiers wanted. In 945 a powerful Persian family, called the **Buyids**, took over Baghdad. The Buyids allowed the caliphs to stay, but they had no real power. They were **puppet rulers**, who had to do as they were told. In 1055 new invaders swept through Syria and Persia. They were the **Seljuk Turks**, Muslims from the north, and their leader, Toghrul Beg, captured Baghdad. He allowed the caliphs to stay in Baghdad, but he took the title of **sultan** (ruler), and kept real power to himself. For 200 years the Abbasid caliphs had to do what they were told by the Seljuks. The Arabic and Persian cultures which had shaped the Muslim world were joined by a Turkish influence.

The end of the Abbasids eventually came in 1258. People from central Asia called the **Mongols** invaded the area. They were led by **Ghengis Khan**, but he died before he could attack Baghdad. It was his grandson, Hulagu, who attacked the city. In a six-day siege, he used flamethrowers to overcome the defenders.

Hulagu

Hulagu (1217–65) was the cruel grandson of Ghengis Khan, the Mongol warrior. Hulagu's Mongol army attacked Persia in 1257. His mounted horsemen were tent dwelling nomads living on mare's milk and horse flesh. He waged war with siege engines, Chinese archers and gunpowder.

In 1258, Hulagu defeated the army of Caliph al-Musta'sim and had Baghdad at his mercy. The caliph was tied in a sack and kicked to death by horses.

Hulagu went on to conquer the rest of the Middle East in similar manner. One Muslim prince who stood in his way, al-Kamil, was forced to eat chunks of his own flesh until he died. Syria and Persia remained in Mongol hands until the Muslim rulers of Egypt, the Mamlukes, recaptured the area for Islam in 1260.

The Abbasids lose control of Muslim lands 750-1258

Muslims conquer Spain	Exiled Umayyad dynasty controls Muslim Spain
711	1031

Abbasid control gradually getting weaker	Tulunite dynasty in control	Fatimid dynasty in control
868	970	

The Umayyads rule from Damascus	Abbasid caliphate starts	Army dominates the Abbasid caliphs	The Buyids control the Abbasid caliphs
750	about 830	945	105●

Hulagu leads the Mongol siege of Baghdad in 1258. From a 15th century Persian manuscript.

When at last the city fell, the caliph was kicked to death and half of the city's two million people were slaughtered, including most of the caliph's family. The irrigation system which watered the fields around Baghdad was destroyed. This meant that the huge city could not be fed. The most glorious time in the history of Baghdad was finished. The Abbasid dynasty had ended.

They came, they uprooted, they burned, they killed, they destroyed, they departed.

A historian from eastern Persia writing about the Mongol invaders in the 13th century.

Various Muslim families control Muslim Spain

Ayyubid dynasty in control	Mamluk dynasty in control

1250

The Seljuk Turks control the Abbasid caliphs	Baghdad destroyed by the Mongols

1258

☐ Events in Spain

☐ Events in Egypt

☐ Events in Baghdad

3.12 The Crusades

For Christians, the area where Christ had lived was called the Holy Land. Bethlehem, Nazareth and Jerusalem were holy places. Ever since the death of Christ, Christians had gone on **pilgrimages**, or journeys there. Some of these holy places are also sacred to Muslims. They believe that Muhammad visited heaven from Jerusalem. The Dome of the Sacred Rock Mosque is there and Jerusalem is the third most holy city in the Muslim world.

The Holy Land was ruled by Christians when Muhammad was alive. After his death, this area was one of the first places the Muslims captured. The Muslim caliphs let the Christian pilgrims carry on visiting the Holy Land.

But in 1055, the Seljuk Turks took control in Baghdad. Their sultans did not treat the Christian pilgrims as well. Many were insulted, attacked and even killed. This made the Christians in Europe very angry. In 1095, the leader of the Christian Church, Pope Urban, made an appeal for Christians to recapture the Holy Land. It would be a pilgrimage and a holy war; a war for the cross, or **Crusade**.

The **First Crusade** set out for the Holy Land in 1096. It was made up of about 50,000 knights, mainly from France. The Crusaders had a 2,000 mile journey by land. They were led by noblemen like Robert of Normandy, William the Conqueror's son. Some went for religious reasons, some for adventure or the chance to win riches. In 1099, they arrived outside the walls of Jerusalem. The Muslims (the Crusaders called them Saracens) defended stoutly. It was over a month before the city walls were crossed. Once inside, the Christian soldiers killed every Muslim they could find.

A **SOURCE**

A 14th century French illustration of the Crusaders attacking Jerusalem.

B **SOURCE**

The Crusaders used huge wooden catapults to fling rocks at the walls. They built towers on wheels to roll close to the walls. One of the siege towers had a huge wooden statue of Jesus strapped to the front. When they broke through, they killed everyone they could find, men, women and children. To them, they were all unbelievers in God's holy city.

The siege of Jerusalem by the Crusaders. Described in 'Core Skills in History Two' by P. W. Gardner and R. Bateman.

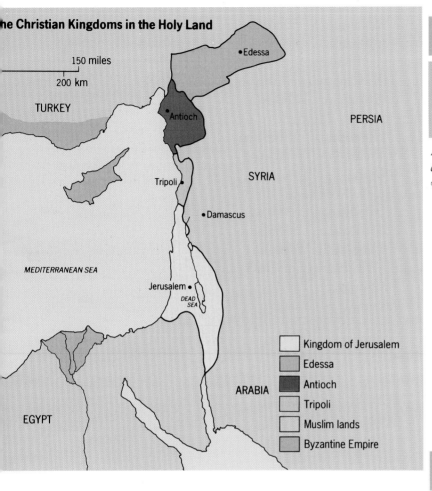

The Christian Kingdoms in the Holy Land

150 miles
200 km

TURKEY

• Edessa

• Antioch

PERSIA

Tripoli •

SYRIA

• Damascus

MEDITERRANEAN SEA

Jerusalem •

DEAD SEA

ARABIA

EGYPT

Kingdom of Jerusalem
Edessa
Antioch
Tripoli
Muslim lands
Byzantine Empire

C

SOURCE

If you take the right path, you will be forgiven all your sins. This path is to make war on the Infidel (non-believers).

An extract from Pope Urban's speech, according to William of Malmesbury who lived at the time.

The Crusaders set up Christian kingdoms in the lands they had captured. These were the kingdoms of Jerusalem, Tripoli, Antioch and Edessa. Parts of these kingdoms lasted for almost 200 years. Naturally the Crusaders and Muslims mixed with each other. The Crusaders were amazed by the quality of the Muslim decorations, carpets, furniture and porcelain. For the first time they enjoyed new foods such as apricots, figs, sugar and lemons. They used cool cotton and silk clothes instead of their own hot woollens. They discovered the use of soap and learned better medical treatments. From Muslim buildings, they learned, for example, how to make pointed arches and pillars which could carry great weights. They also learned how to defend castles by using round towers and **machicolations**. These were narrow gaps in the walls which allowed defenders to shoot arrows or drop rocks on attackers. The Muslims had very little to gain from the Crusaders apart from increased trade with Italy and improved weapons and armour.

D

SOURCE

Our men entered the city, chasing the Saracens into Solomon's Temple and killing them so that all the Temple was streaming with their blood. Our men rushed round the city seizing gold and silver, horses and all sorts of goods. Then they all came rejoicing to worship at the Church of the Holy Sepulcre. Next morning, they went up to the Temple roof, where many were hiding, and cut off their heads. Many Saracens committed suicide by throwing themselves off the roof.

A medieval Christian manuscript, the 'Gesta Francorum', describing the capture of Jerusalem.

In 1144 Edessa was recaptured by the Muslims. The **Second Crusade** came from Europe to try to get it back, but failed. Then, in 1187, a new Muslim leader called **Saladin** attacked the Christian kingdoms. First he defeated the Christians at the Battle of Hattin. He ordered all of the Christian soldiers who survived to be put to death. He then recaptured Jerusalem. The Muslim soldiers celebrated. They wanted to kill all of the Christians inside, but he refused to let them. The **Third Crusade** was sent to drive Saladin out of the Holy Land. One of its leaders was Richard I of England, **Richard the Lionheart**. There were several bloody battles, but Saladin's army was too strong. All Richard could do was to make a truce with Saladin in 1192. This allowed the Christians to live in the cities, like Acre, on the Mediterranean coast and visit the holy places. During the next hundred years the Muslims gradually recaptured the Christian cities. Several new crusades were sent to help them, but all failed. In 1291 the last of the Christian cities fell. The Crusades had failed.

E **SOURCE**

We who were once Westerners are now Easterners. A man may possess here his own houses just as if he had inherited them from his father; another may have taken him a wife, a Syrian or even a baptised Saracen, and live together with all his wife's clan. He who was once a stranger is now a native.

A historian called Fulcher of Chartres, who went on the First Crusade and lived for a while in the Kingdom of Jerusalem.

F **SOURCE**

A game of chess between a Crusader and a Saracen.

The gateway to an Arab desert palace, built near Damascus in about 730.

The gatehouse of Rockingham Castle.

Saladin

Saladin (1137–93) was the most famous of the Muslims who defended their lands against the Crusaders. During his youth, no single Muslim leader could control the whole of the Islamic world. But in 1171, Saladin overthrew the Fatimid leaders of Egypt and founded a new dynasty called the Ayyubids. Soon, his armies spread his control across a huge area stretching from Egypt to Syria.

This area included the lands where Jesus had lived, recently captured by the Crusaders. But these lands were also holy to Muslims, so Saladin joined the jihad, or holy war, to drive the Christian invaders out. He recaptured Jerusalem in 1187.

Muslim historians describe 'Salah ad-Din' as a powerful, yet kind, man. Ibn al-Athir tells how Saladin took a sword and personally cut off the head of the captured Prince Raynard, saying, 'This man once tried to attack Mecca and broke a truce to attack an unarmed Muslim caravan.' Another story tells how Saladin learned that a young couple inside a castle he was attacking were to be married. He delayed the attack. The bride's mother sent out food and Saladin's troops shared in the celebrations.

By 1192, Saladin had seen off the Third Crusade led by Richard I of England. 'I will return in three years to conquer the Holy Land,' wrote Richard to Saladin. 'If I must lose the Holy Land, there is no one to whom I would rather lose it than the English King,' replied Saladin, typically chivalrous. But Richard never returned. Only one year later, Saladin caught a chill, became feverish, fell into a coma, then died.

4.1 Re-shaping the Muslim World

Unit 3.11 showed how the Abbasids lost control of the Muslim world. Arab control stretching from China to the Atlantic Ocean would never reappear. Instead, the Muslim world was divided up, as different parts were conquered by different invaders. New empires emerged. Some only lasted a few years, but others lasted for centuries. Islam survived all of this. The invaders became Muslims and their empires were Muslim too.

Most of these empires were set up by invasions of people from the east. They were the **Mongol-Tartar** people from the barren wastes of central Asia. They were fierce warriors, nomads who lived in tents and fought on horseback. From about the year 1000 they came sweeping across Asia into the wealthy cities of the Muslim world. At first, they destroyed cities and massacred their people. But as the warriors were joined by settlers, they built up the cities again and created rich new empires.

The Turks were one group of these people. The **Seljuk Turks** captured Baghdad in 1055. The **Ayyubids** and the **Mamlukes** were Turks who captured Egypt. They were the first to take power over the Muslim world from the Arabs and Persians. (See pages 38–39.)

Then the **Mongols** attacked, led by **Ghenghis Khan**. They destroyed Baghdad in 1258 and captured most of the Middle East. Later, a rival Mongol invader appeared in 1369. This was Timur the Lame, sometimes called **Tamerlane**. He ruled an empire based around Samarkand. But Tamerlane's empire did not last long after his death.

In 1502 a new empire grew up in Persia led by Ismail Safavi. This **Safavid** empire lasted until about 1720. Further east, another Mongol, **Babur**, captured most of India and set up an empire which was to last until the 19th century. This is known as the **Mughal Empire**.

However, we are going to look at just one of the new empires. It was an empire started by Turks. It grew up in Asia Minor in about 1300 under the Turkish leader Osman. The empire was named after him and it lasted until about 1920. It was the **Ottoman Empire**. The rest of this book is about the Ottomans.

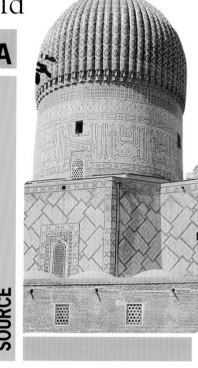

A SOURCE

The Gur Emir, built by Tamerlane and finished in 1434. It houses his tomb.

B SOURCE

Miniature painting showing an elephant being used in battle.

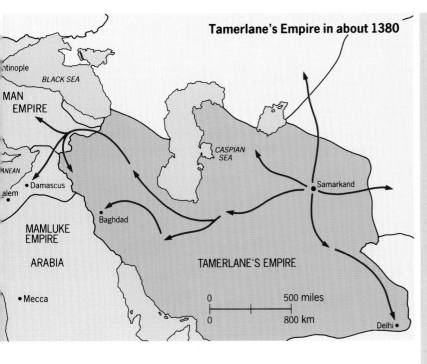

Tamerlane's Empire in about 1380

BLACK SEA

ntinople

MAN
EMPIRE

NEAN

alem
• Damascus

CASPIAN
SEA

Baghdad

Samarkand

MAMLUKE
EMPIRE

ARABIA

TAMERLANE'S EMPIRE

• Mecca

0		500 miles
0		800 km

Delhi •

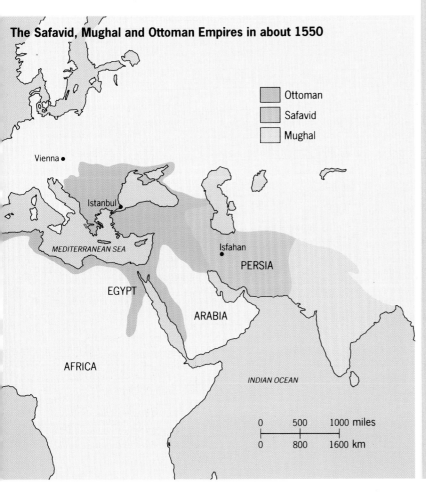

The Safavid, Mughal and Ottoman Empires in about 1550

Ottoman
Safavid
Mughal

Vienna •

Istanbul •

MEDITERRANEAN SEA

Isfahan •

PERSIA

EGYPT

ARABIA

AFRICA

INDIAN OCEAN

0	500	1000 miles
0	800	1600 km

Tamerlane was born in 1336. He became the ruler of his homeland of Turkestan. His people called him Timur, but he had an illness called gout which gave him a limp and thus he became known as 'Timur the Lame'. In the West, this became Tamerlane. His capital was at Samarkand. From 1369 his armies invaded Russia, India and Persia. He destroyed many cities and murdered their people. It is said that after his capture of Delhi he had the skulls of 80,000 victims piled up outside the city gates. But he was also interested in the arts and he built as many beautiful buildings as he destroyed. Muslim building at this time is famous for the large areas of walls decorated with highly-coloured tiles. (See Source A.)

Ismail Safavi declared himself shah in 1502. The **Safavids** built up a Persian Empire which lasted until about 1720. Shah Abbas (1587–1629) was the greatest of all the Safavid rulers. Under the Safavids, with their capital at Isfahan, the Shi'ite sect became dominant in Iran. It still is. Also at this time Persian artists created the best miniatures in Islamic history. (See Source B.) Miniatures are small paintings used to decorate books.

Babur was a Mongol prince descended from Tamerlane. In 1526 his armies conquered India and set up a new Muslim empire with its capital at Delhi. It is known as the **Mughal Empire**. The fourth Mughal emperor, Shah Jahan, built the most famous Muslim shrine in the world. When his wife died giving birth to their child, he built the Taj Mahal in her memory.

4.2 Rise of the Ottoman Empire

In about 1300 a group of Muslim Turks in Anatolia (present-day Turkey) started to attack their neighbours to get more land for themselves. They were led by **Osman** (sometimes known as Othman). They attacked other Turks and also the Christian Byzantine Empire. A series of warlike sultans followed Osman; they became known as the Ottomans. In 1451 **Mehmet II** became the Ottoman sultan. His ambition was to capture **Constantinople**, the capital of the Byzantine Empire.

Mehmet prepared carefully and in 1453, he launched his attack. The siege of Constantinople lasted six weeks. Barbaro, a soldier from Venice who escaped, said that so many defenders were killed that the heads floating in the sea reminded him of melons floating in the canals of Venice. But Mehmet ordered that the buildings should be spared. He renamed the city **Istanbul** and made it his capital. He built new palaces, schools, hospitals and mosques. Istanbul was to become the splendid centre of the world's biggest Muslim empire for 450 years.

A 15th century map of Constantinople.

A 16th century miniature painting showing Mehmet II leading his troops into Constantinople.

C Constantinople had the sea on two sides and, on the west, a land wall. Once it had controlled the seas all around the city. But now the Ottomans had built two naval bases in the Bosphorus so that their ships could cut off food supplies. Mehmet II massed his troops on the land side. He had at least 150,000 men and enormous cannons. One took 60 oxen to move and 200 men to hold it on its wagon.

The city had three lines of walls: the inner wall was 40 feet high with towers; a second wall ran parallel to and outside it; the third wall was the stone facing of the foss (ditch) around the city. The defenders massed around the second wall, because the inner wall was in a bad state of repair. They numbered about 7,000 men. A great chain went across the Golden Horn to protect the city harbour.

From 12 April onwards, the Turkish guns bombarded the city walls and the Turkish soldiers tried to fill in the foss. Great gaps appeared in the walls. Mehmet's engineers managed to bring ships overland from the Bosphorus. On 22 April, 70 Turkish ships appeared in the Golden Horn.

Mehmet keyed up his forces for a final assault on 29 May. About an hour after midnight the attack began: first the Bashi-Bazouks, then the Anatolian Turks and finally the janissaries, who eventually gained access to the city.

SOURCE

Extracts from the work of a modern historian writing in 'The Rise of Islam', 1969.

D Previous sieges failed because the city was supplied by sea. But Mehmet built naval forts, to help his ships. When access for his 125 vessels into the Golden Horn was blocked, the fleet was hauled overland. On land, cannon tore into the city walls; the 7,000 defending troops beat back the Turks. But the cannon breached the walls and they poured through.

SOURCE

From 'Religion at the Crossroads' by J. Milton, R. Steinberg and S. Lewis, 1980.

E

Constantinople during the siege of 1453

Rumeli Hisar (naval fort)
Anadolu Hisar (naval fort)
Bashi-Bazouks
Sultan's tent
Janissaries
Anatolian Turks
Golden Horn
The chain
BOSPHORUS
City walls

0   1   2 miles
0 1 2 3 km

SOURCE

Mehmet II

Mehmet II (1432–81), also known as Mohammed II or Mohammed the Conqueror, was a linguist, poet, supporter of the arts, student of Oriental and Greek philosophy, gardener and superb horseman and archer.

He is best known for his war successes. His armies captured Constantinople, Serbia, Albania, Herzegovina, Bosnia and much of Greece. Even the wealthy state of Venice paid tributes to him to bribe him not to attack them. When he died, Mehmet left his people wallowing in power, and grumbling about taxation, after a reign spent mainly at war.

4.3 Expansion of the Ottoman Empire

The Ottomans used fear to help them expand their empire. (See Source A.) But fear alone was not enough. The cream of the Ottoman army was the **janissaries**. They were Christians, captured as boys, who had converted to Islam and then trained as elite soldiers. They were the sultan's personal slaves, fighting for Allah. They were not allowed to marry or own property, so the army was their life. The janissaries could always be recognized in battle by their white headgear. Originally they were archers, but later they were issued with handguns. No other Muslim army had such advanced weapons. The Ottoman Empire also became a great naval power. It paid the fierce **Barbary pirates** from North Africa to fight for the empire. They terrorized the southern coasts of Europe and dominated the Mediterranean. Their leader, Barbarossa, became the admiral of the Turkish fleet. His ships were more mobile than those used in Europe. He brought back to Istanbul treasure and riches plundered from the ports and ships of the West.

At first the Ottomans used this military might to attack Europe. After Constantinople, **Mehmet II** conquered Athens and the Greek peninsula, Albania, the area around the Black Sea and the whole of Anatolia. By 1477 he had captured Bosnia and was on the verge of capturing Italy. The Christian European states rarely got together to oppose the Muslims. But Mehmet died in 1481 and the Ottomans became involved in wars against the Safavids.

The Safavids were Shi'ite Muslims from Persia. They had tried to convert Muslims to the Shi'ite sect all across the Middle East. The Ottomans were orthodox Sunni Muslims. Sultan **Selim I** (1512–20) declared a holy war against the Safavids. He drove them back into Persia and captured Iraq and Syria. Victories here were easier than in Europe. His armies swept on to capture Egypt from the Mamlukes. Within eight years, Selim doubled the size of the Ottoman Empire.

A **SOURCE**

Murad I combined military brilliance with brutality. Capturing Chorlu, halfway between Adrianople and Constantinople, he ordered the garrison to be massacred and its commander beheaded. This so terrified the people of Adrianople that they gave up the city without a fight.

From 'Religion at the Crossroads' by J. Milton, R. Steinberg and S. Lewis, 1980.

B **SOURCE**

Suleiman the Magnificent and his army defeating the Hungarians at the Battle of Mohács in 1526. Notice the white plumed headgear of the janissaries.

C

SOURCE

An Ottoman galley used Christian slaves chained to the oars, and also had sails.

Barbarossa

Barbarossa (about 1466–1546) was a Muslim pirate from the Barbary Coast of North Africa. His Arabic name was Khair ed-Din; he was called Barbarossa for his red beard. He led a fleet terrorizing the Mediterranean. He fought for any ruler who would pay, like the King of France, the Holy Roman Emperor and Charles V. He fought mainly for Sultan Suleiman. He captured Algiers in 1519, Tunis in 1534. In 1536, he became admiral of the Turkish fleet. Their naval control lasted until their defeat by the Christians at Lepanto in 1571.

But the greatest Ottoman sultan was still to come. Selim's son, **Suleiman**, became sultan in 1520. He captured Belgrade in 1521, Rhodes in 1522, then the whole of the north coast of Africa. In 1529 Suleiman seemed set to capture Vienna in the heart of Europe. But bad weather reduced the food for his men and horses and made the roads impassable for his cannon. He turned back and again Europe was spared. The map on this page shows how the Ottomans towered over the western world by the time of Suleiman's death in 1566.

The growth of the Ottoman Empire up to 1566

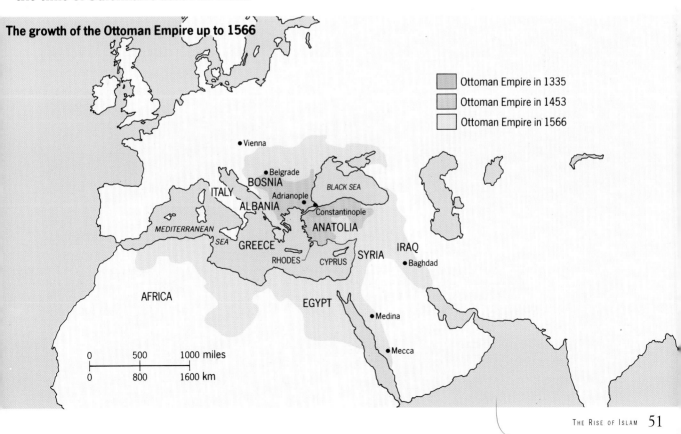

Ottoman Empire in 1335
Ottoman Empire in 1453
Ottoman Empire in 1566

Vienna • Belgrade • BOSNIA • ITALY • ALBANIA • Adrianople • BLACK SEA • Constantinople • ANATOLIA • MEDITERRANEAN SEA • GREECE • RHODES • CYPRUS • SYRIA • IRAQ • Baghdad • AFRICA • EGYPT • Medina • Mecca

0   500   1000 miles
0   800   1600 km

4.4 Life at the Ottoman Court

The sultan lived a life of luxury. Most of the court officials were his personal slaves. His gardeners would fill the grounds of the palace with fine flowers, rare birds and wild animals. For amusement he would go hawking or call for his slave wrestlers, jugglers and dancers. The sultan also had a **harem**. The women of the harem were slaves selected for their beauty and brains. No men entered the harem apart from the sultan, his sons and the black eunuchs who acted as guards. None of the women was ever allowed to leave the harem.

But the sultan also had the business of government to attend to. His power was total but he had advisers. His most important official was the **grand vizier**, and his council of advisers was the **divan**. Suleiman the Magnificent's divan would meet every morning as a court, to hear complaints against people and pass judgment. In the afternoon it would meet to discuss government policy. Each of the advisers had hundreds of officials and clerks to help him collect taxes and apply the laws. All of these officials, from the grand vizier down, were slaves. They were educated in the palace schools and were totally loyal to the sultan.

A **SOURCE**

The slave who dressed Suleiman put 20 gold ducats in the pockets of his master's silk caftan every morning and was rewarded with the robe and the remaining coins at night.

From 'Religion at the Crossroads' by J. Milton, R. Steinberg, and S. Lewis, 1980.

A miniature painting showing the sultan visiting his harem.

B **SOURCE**

C

Two of the punishments used by the Ottoman courts.

Suleiman

Suleiman the Magnificent (1494–1566) was sultan from 1520–66. His armies captured Belgrade in 1521, Rhodes in 1522 and Hungary in 1526. Vienna, in the heart of Europe, was besieged in 1529. How different European history might have been if he had conquered Austria. Suleiman fell under the influence of Roxalana, a slave in his harem. He broke tradition, allowing his concubines into the court. Bribery and deceit grew to get the support of the sultan's favourite slave girls. By the time that Suleiman died, intrigue in the court was rife.

Away from the capital, there was a network of judges, called **qadis**. These were **ulema**, respected Muslims who had studied the laws of Islam. The Koran was their guide. No one could be punished without their permission, although non-Muslims were tried and punished by their own leaders. Ottoman punishments were very harsh; amputation of a hand for horse stealing, for example. But the Koran allowed harsh punishments. The law was harsh in other parts of the world at that time too. In England, Elizabeth I was on the throne and English punishments were just as severe. The Ottomans had no police force to keep order, they had to rely on fear.

D

The grand vizier chairs a meeting of the sultan's council. The sultan can be seen observing from behind the window at the back.

4.5 Life in the Ottoman Empire

Trade was an important part of the Ottoman Empire. Every city had its **bedestan**, or bazaar. This was the market place where goods from all over the world were bought and sold. The people of the cities depended on the traders for their food and other goods. In Mehmet II's reign the bedestan in Istanbul had over 1,000 stalls. Buyers would haggle over prices. This is still the custom in the market places of the Muslim world. The Ottomans copied the Arab **caravansaries** along the overland trade routes. Caravansaries were fortified stopping places for traders. The sultans wanted to encourage trade so they allowed free food and lodgings for three days to all traders. One great caravansary contained 200 rooms and a courtyard big enough for 5,000 horses.

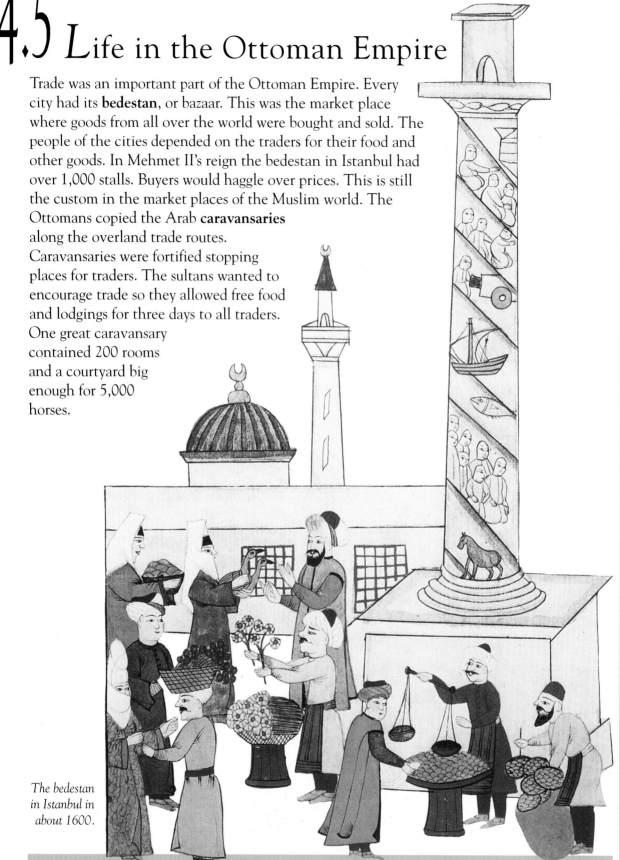

The bedestan in Istanbul in about 1600.

The profits of trade made the traders wealthy. But they weren't the only ones to benefit. Muslims give some of their income to charity every year. Hospitals often grew up around the bedestan, funded by gifts. The sultans also charged the traders taxes. Mehmet II needed taxes to build up his new capital of Istanbul. He encouraged skilled craftsmen to settle in the city, promising them safety and lower taxes. The Venetian painter Bellini spent a year in Istanbul. The palace schools also produced artists, poets and architects. Many of these craftsmen were used to convert the Christian churches of Constantinople into mosques. Their changes were sometimes simple, but often they added splendid decoration.

Outside the palace, there were also **medreses**, or free schools, for Muslim boys. Suleiman paid for many of these out of income from taxes. Each school was attached to a mosque and taught the ideas of Islam, grammar, geometry and astronomy. Colleges taught the more gifted students when they were older. This was the time of the Renaissance in Europe, when learning and art flourished. But no European capital could match the thriving city of Istanbul for learning and culture.

C

SOURCE

The Hagia Sophia was a splendid Christian church in Constantinople when the Turks captured it in 1453. The Ottomans converted it to a mosque. This is one of the panels altered by the Muslim craftsmen.

Mustafa Celebi

Mustafa Celebi was a Turkish trader in the 16th century. Little is known about traders in Baghdad's Bedestan, but Mustafa Celebi's name appears in Ottoman records. In 1577, he was given a monopoly of the Sultan's fur trade with the Russian traders around Moscow. He was sent with 4000 gold ducats to buy furs. His work as a trader made him wealthy enough to wear robes decorated by the furs he brought to Baghdad.

B

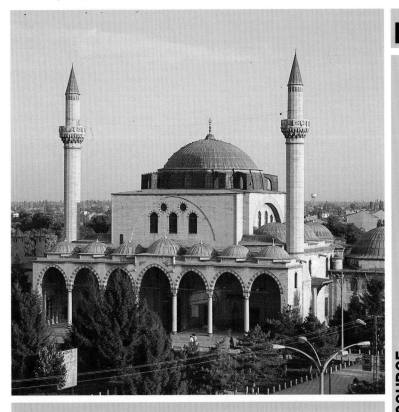

SOURCE

The mosque of Selim II, built in Konya, Turkey in 1575.

4.6 Decline of the Ottoman Empire

The early Ottoman sultans were talented generals and rulers. From the end of Suleiman's reign the sultans were less able.

Suleiman had broken with custom and taken as one of his four legal wives **Roxelana**, a Russian slave girl from the harem. She convinced Suleiman that his oldest son was plotting to overthrow him. Suleiman ordered him to be strangled. So it was Roxelana's son, **Selim II**, who became the next sultan, in 1566. He was short and fat, had no training or liking for government or war, and drank so much that he was known as **Selim the Sot**. He relied totally on his grand vizier.

Selim knew that the island of Cyprus was famed for its wine. In 1571 he ordered his grand vizier to capture it. But a huge fleet of ships from Europe gathered to defend the island. The ships met at the **Battle of Lepanto**. The Ottomans suffered their first major defeat.

A modern historian writing in 'The Rise of Islam', 1969.

A

SOURCE

A painting of Suleiman painted in Europe in the 16th century by Hans Eworth.

By this time the Ottoman Empire had expanded as far as it could. The army could only fight in the spring and summer. By the time it got to the borders of the empire it was too late for a long campaign against new cities. So the conquests stopped.

In 1574 Selim II, drunk on Cyprus wine, slipped in a bath and cracked his skull. Over the next 140 years, thirteen sultans followed. None had the ability of the first Ottoman sultans. Many of them were overthrown in plots. When Mehmet III came to the throne in 1595 he took no chances. He murdered all nineteen of his brothers. Everyone feared for their life. It was impossible to rule under these conditions.

The Ottoman Empire lasted for 350 years like this. It was still huge, with a population of 30 million, but it was weak. It became known as 'The Sick Man of Europe'. It was bullied by other countries and its provinces ignored the orders of the sultans. The last Ottoman sultan was deposed in 1922.

C

SOURCE

The sultans so completely lacked the strong, warlike, dedicated spirit of the first sultans that some historians have doubted whether Selim II really was Suleiman's son. Many of them were cowards, at least one was an imbecile, others were corrupt. Only a few able grand viziers saved the empire.

The janissaries took power into their own hands. They conspired to get the throne for their favourite prince – and then charged him huge sums for their support. They opened their ranks for other Muslims to enrol as janissaries, without the training. The system of the most able slaves getting the best positions in government ended. People started to buy jobs with bribes.

Government funds declined as trade declined and fewer conquests meant less plunder.

From 'Religion at the Crossroads' by J. Milton, R. Steinberg and S. Lewis, 1980.

Selim II

Selim II (1524–74), sometimes known as Selim the Sot or Selim the Drunkard, was the Ottoman sultan for eight years. He became sultan at the death of his famous father, Suleiman the Magnificent, in 1566. Even while Suleiman was alive, Selim and his brother Bayezid fought each other for the right to succeed to the throne. In 1559, Selim defeated his brother's army at Konya. Bayezid fled to Persia, but was captured and sent back to Selim.

To settle the succession, Bayezid was strangled with a bowstring, as were his five sons, the youngest aged only three. Selim had no interest in running his empire. He left this to his grand vizier, Sokollu. He died of a fever after hitting his skull when falling down drunk in a Turkish bath.

A 16th century painting of Selim II.

D

SOURCE

5.1 Architecture

The Arabs learned about building from others. They adopted domes and pillars from the Roman and Greek styles of the Byzantine Empire. They took the pointed arch from the Persians. But **minarets** (the tall towers seen on mosques) were developed by the Arabs themselves. Their main efforts went into religious buildings, like mosques and mausoleums (tombs). But they also built schools, universities and fortresses which still survive.

The Arabs developed a clear style in their buildings. They set the pattern for other Muslim architects all over the world. They also learned design and engineering skills so they could build large buildings. Builders in Europe copied these when building their castles and cathedrals.

B

SOURCE

The minaret of the Koutoubia Mosque at Marrakesh in Morocco. Built in the 12th century by the Arabs.

A

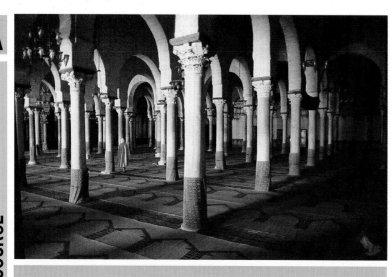

SOURCE

The prayer room of the Great Mosque at Kairouan in Tunisia. This mosque was built by the Arabs in the 7th century.

C

Mosques need not be covered. Worship can take place in open courtyards. Every mosque will have somewhere for worshippers to wash before prayer. There are no pews or benches inside. Everyone prays on the floor, which is usually covered by carpet. There are no pictures or statues inside. This is to avoid any hint of idol worship. A domed roof represents the universe and the minaret allows the muezzin to climb up and call Muslims to prayer.

SOURCE

From 'Islamic Worship' by R. Bruce, 1985.

SOURCE

The Blue Mosque, started in 1609 by the Muslim Ottoman Turks, in Constantinople.

SOURCE

Regents Park Mosque.

E

SOURCE

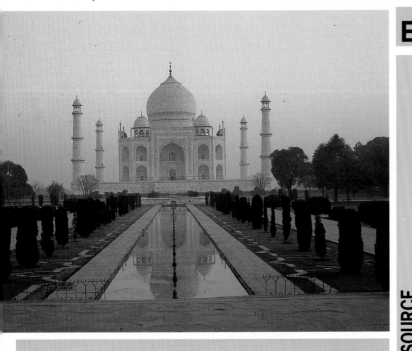

The Taj Mahal at Agra in India. Built in about 1635 by the Muslim Mughal ruler Shah Jahan as a mausoleum for his favourite wife who died in childbirth.

Mumtaz Mahal

Arjumand Bano Begum (about 1592–1631) was renamed Mumtaz Mahal ('the prize of the palace') in 1612 when she married Prince Khurram, son of the Mughal Emperor, Jahangir. Her husband later became the Emperor Shah Jahan.

They were happily married. She bore him fourteen children. When she died, aged 39, he ordered a monument in her memory to be built on the River Jumna's banks at Agra. It took 22 years to build. When it was finished, her body was moved to the most majestic monument, the Taj Mahal.

5.2 The Impact of Islam (2)

The rise of Islam has left its mark on the world.

From about 700, the Muslims gathered the knowledge of the Ancient Greeks from old books. They also learned from China and India. It was only after about 1300 that Europe became interested in all this knowledge. Many of the Greek books had disappeared for ever by then. But the knowledge was not lost. Source A shows how Europe learned from the Muslims.

The Muslims also made a more obvious mark on Europe. Islands like Rhodes, Cyprus, and Sicily were all occupied by the Arabs for a while. A large part of Spain was Muslim for over 700 years. The buildings, the language, the food and the music of these places still show Muslim influence. The Muslim traders also spread their religion outside Europe and the Middle East. Indonesia, in the Far East, has a Muslim population of almost 150 million people today.

A page from the 'Canon of Medicine', written by the Persian doctor Avicenna in 1000. Doctors in Europe used this book until about 1800.

But the biggest impact was on people's lives inside the Muslim world. This huge area was not only united by Islam the religion; it was also united by Islamic society and culture.

The **religious unity** meant that all over this area the Five Pillars of Islam became the centre of people's lives. The belief in one God, daily prayers, acts of charity, fasting and pilgrimages were all shared by millions of Muslims. The Koran was the same in Tunisia as it was in India.

But Islam is not just a religion; it is a way of life. So the whole of **society** changed. Islam had rules about the food people could eat, the way they should dress, the role of women. Islam insisted on fair treatment for all races and all religions. Christians and Jews, for example, were normally treated well. Not all cultures have been so tolerant. Polygamy was strengthened. Gambling and charging interest for lending money were frowned upon. Alcoholic drinks were banned.

People's **culture** changed too. More people lived in towns. Cities grew up where villages had been before. They had mosques with open courtyards, minarets, arches and domes. Their other buildings copied some of these features. Fountains and gardens became more common. Art also changed. The Muslims used tiles for decoration more than any other society. And everywhere Arabic, the language of the Koran, became the common language.

By 1550 this was the Islamic civilization. Today, the lives of the world's 1,100,000,000 Muslims still show the impact of the changes made then.

A Muslim funeral in modern Spain.

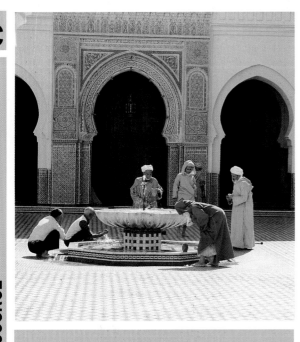

Muslims outside a mosque in modern Morocco.

Avicenna

Ibn-Sina (980–1037), known as Avicenna in the West, was an Arab doctor, philosopher, poet and astronomer. He was born in Bukhara, then part of the Persian Empire. By the age of 20 he was seen as the most learned man of his time. He is a typical example of the Arab Muslim scholars who taught the West a great deal.

His *Canon of Medicine* was over one million words in length. It came from his study of the Ancient Greek scholars, Hippocrates and Galen. He described lockjaw, pleurisy and treatment for malaria. He understood that tuberculosis was contagious and described his oral anaesthetics and animal experiments. In all, he wrote almost 100 books on theology, philosophy, astronomy, science, medicine and poetry. Avicenna was buried at Hamadhan, in modern Iran. A shrine, built in his honour, was reconstructed in 1954.

5.3 The Challenge for Islam Today

By 1600 the Ottoman Turks were weak. Other countries took over parts of their Muslim empire. By 1900 Britain, France and Italy ruled most of north Africa. At the end of the First World War in 1918 the Turks were punished for supporting Germany. Britain and France took over all of the Arab lands still in the Ottoman Empire. It has only been in the last 40 years that these lands have been allowed to rule themselves again with their own Muslim governments.

Oil has made some Arab countries very rich and powerful since the early 1970s. Some Muslims want to use their wealth to become more like people in the West. People in Europe and the USA enjoy a high standard of living. But other Muslims don't trust the West. They see western culture as evil, where gambling, alcohol and sexual freedom are allowed. Some countries, like Turkey, have relaxed Islamic rules and have become very westernized. But others, like Saudi Arabia and Iran, want to get back to the strict basics of Islam. Their rules on alcohol and punishment, for example, are very rigid.

A

SOURCE

What I refuse to do is abandon Islamic principles. We do not cut off the hand of any who steal to eat. Anyone under such necessity is not to blame. Only he who steals for stealing's sake is open to this penalty. Take another case, adultery. There is no question of stoning the adulterer or adulteress as has been falsely claimed. The punishment is flogging, 100 lashes.

Colonel Gadafi, leader of Libya, quoted by M. Bianco, 'Gadafi, Voice of the Desert', 1975.

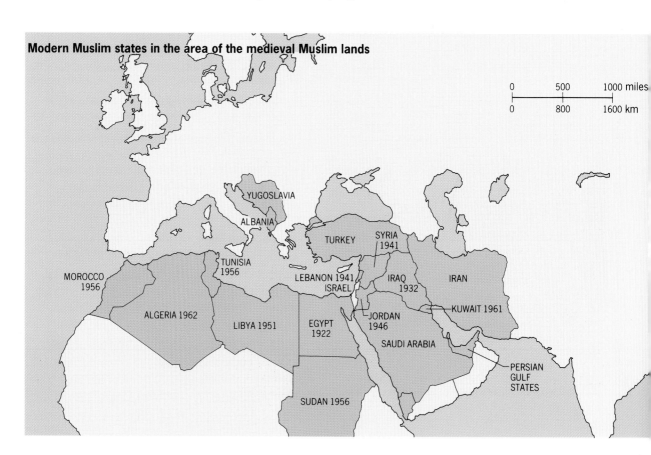

Modern Muslim states in the area of the medieval Muslim lands

YUGOSLAVIA

ALBANIA

TURKEY

SYRIA 1941

TUNISIA 1956

LEBANON 1941
ISRAEL

IRAQ 1932

IRAN

MOROCCO 1956

KUWAIT 1961

ALGERIA 1962

JORDAN 1946

LIBYA 1951

EGYPT 1922

SAUDI ARABIA

PERSIAN GULF STATES

SUDAN 1956

0   500   1000 miles
0   800   1600 km

This has caused tensions. Muslims argue with other Muslims about what they should do. The split between Sunni and Shi'ite Muslims continues. Some Muslims living in non-Muslim countries demand different schools or different food. The people around them often don't understand. This causes confusion and sometimes anger and violence. There have also been tensions between Muslim and non-Muslim countries.

Muslims have a glorious past. Creating a place for Islam in the modern world sometimes causes problems. This makes it vital that the world understands Islam. We hope this book has helped.

An illustration from a Muslim book, 'Islam, Beliefs and Teachings', by the Muslim Educational Trust, 1984.

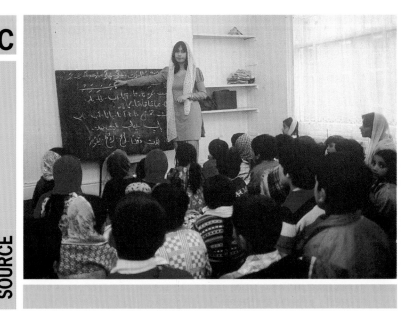

Muslim children in an Islamic school in Nelson, Lancashire.

Muslim women in the modern world: one solution for a young doctor in South Yemen!

Gaddafi

Colonel Gaddafi (1942–) is the modern day leader of Libya in North Africa. In the West, the media often depict him as a trouble-maker and terrorist. He believes that all Muslim countries should be free from Western interference. His Muslim supporters say that he should be given the credit for basing the laws of Libya on the laws in the Koran.

For example, Gaddafi is keen to base penalties for breaking the law on the punishments laid down in the Koran. Thieves have had their hands cut off in public. Adulterers have suffered 100 lashes. Some of these punishments may seem unduly cruel to Western eyes.